IN SEARCH OF

Britain's Haunted Castles

Marc Alexander and Paul Abrahams

Warwick Castle.

First published 2012

The History Press
The Mill, Brimscombe Port,
Stroud, Gloucestershire, GL5 2QG
www.thehistorypress.co.uk

British Library Cataloguing in Publication Data.
A catalogue record for this book is available from the British Library.

ISBN 978 0 7524 6454 1

Typesetting and origination by The History Press
Printed in Great Britain

CONTENTS

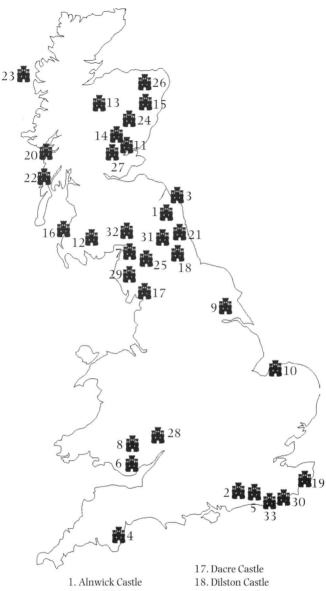

1. Alnwick Castle
2. Arundel Castle
3. Bamburgh Castle
4. Berry Pomeroy Castle
5. Bramber Castle
6. Caerphilly Castle
7. Carlisle Castle
8. Castell Coch
9. Cawood Castle
10. Castle Rising
11. Claypotts Castle
12. Closeburn Castle
13. Corgarff Castle
14. Cortachy Castle
15. Crathes Castle
16. Culzean Castle

17. Dacre Castle
18. Dilston Castle
19. Dover Castle
20. Dunstaffnage Castle
21. Dunstanburgh Castle
22. Duntrune Castle
23. Dunvegan Castle
24. Edzell Castle
25. Featherstone Castle
26. Fyvie Castle
27. Glamis Castle
28. Goodrich Castle
29. Greystoke Castle
30. Hastings Castle
31. Haughton Castle
32. Hermitage Castle
33. Herstmonceaux Castle

INTRODUCTION

In Italy when a traditional ghost story is told it often begins with the words '*C'era una volta un castello in Cornovaglia* ... ('There was once a castle in Cornwall ...). Such an opening indicates that Britain's reputation for its ghostlore remains as intriguing as ever. This book is for those interested in ghostlore – and castles – and for those who wish to visit the scenes of paranormal legend.

The length of the entries varies greatly. The reason is that the wordage reflects what is known about the haunting. For example, some sites are merely haunted by an anonymous white lady whose story has long been forgotten. There is little that can be written about her. On the other hand, many castles have spectres that go back far in history and their stories are well documented, such as the case of a man found guilty of murder on evidence based on trial and the appearance of an apparition at Cawood Castle.

A number of haunted castles have royal ghosts which is not surprising when one considers the role of the castle in British history. No one realised the potential of the castle more than William the Conqueror. In 1066 he brought six prefabricated wooden castles across the Channel, and as soon as he was King of England began building castles to control the subject population and hold back the undefeated Celts of Wales and Scotland. Through castles William's feudal system was maintained.

To the conquered Saxons the new Norman motte and bailey castles – built on earthen mounds with protected courtyards – must have appeared as bitter symbols of oppression, especially when the first hurriedly erected wooden fortifications were replaced with frowning stone keeps. But apart from being a symbol of oppression, the castle also offered security to the local population when the baron's cavalry rode out across the drawbridge to counter reivers and bandits.

But in times of anarchy, such as in the reign of King Stephen, masters of castles could become laws unto themselves – as noted by the authors of the *Anglo-Saxon Chronicle*:

> Every powerful man built his castles and held them against him (the king) and they filled the country full of castles. They oppressed the wretched people of the country severely with castle building.

> When the castles were built they filled them with devils and wicked men. Then both by night and by day they took those people they thought had any goods both men and women, put them in prison and tortured with indescribable torture to extort gold and silver … I have neither the ability nor the power to tell all the horrors or all the torments then inflicted upon the wretched people in this country. And that lasted nineteen years while Stephen was king, and it was always going from bad to worse.

It is of little wonder that many castles became haunted.

In this book the question as to what ghosts are, or even if they exist, does not arise. The fact that down the centuries thousands of people have believed in them is enough and, in order to avoid the boring repetition, words and expressions referring to ghostly manifestations in castles as 'reputed', 'alleged', 'it is claimed', or 'some say' are omitted. Here ghosts are written about as factual. Disbelief is suspended and phantoms do walk castle walls and re-enact tragedies.

Many of the castles mentioned in these pages are open to the public. Because opening times can vary or be cancelled – for building work or special functions, for example – it is advisable to check when planning specific visits, especially if a long journey is involved. As most castles open to the public have websites, up-to-date information is easily available on the internet. Ruins that do not need a permanent custodian may be visited at any reasonable time.

Castles on private land, or closed to the public, can still be viewed from road or path without invading the privacy of their residents – but it must not be forgotten that an Englishman's castle is often his home.

Marc Alexander & Paul Abrahams, 2012

Unless otherwise stated, all photographs were taken by the authors.

ALNWICK CASTLE

Today Alnwick Castle retains an aura of magic due to being portrayed as Hogwarts in the Harry Potter films. It is a castle that one would expect to be haunted as stretching back through its long history nine of its lords have died in violent or mysterious circumstances. Yet it was not a spectral knight or white lady who frightened those who once lived under its shadow – it was something much more terrifying.

Guarding the Border town of the same name, the castle is often referred to as 'The Windsor of the North' and is the home of the Duke and Duchess of Northumberland. Its origins go back almost a thousand years to when Gilbert de Tesson, who had been Duke William's standard-bearer at the Battle of Hastings, became the first Norman master of the region. After he rebelled against William Rufus, the site passed to Yvo de Vescy who began to build a fortification there as a protection against Scottish raiders.

The present castle was begun by his son-in-law, Eustace Fitzjohn, in 1140. It was attacked on several occasions by the Scots, and in 1403 Henry IV captured it when its then owner, Henry Percy, rebelled against him. It was besieged again in 1462 during the Wars of the Roses but escaped the attentions of both sides in the Civil War due to its owner's neutral policy.

In 1755 the 1st Duke of Northumberland commissioned Robert Adam to restore it and it is to him it owes its Gothic appearance and the lead statues stationed on the battlements which are such a striking feature today.

The being that once terrorised Alnwick was one of the rarest found in British folklore – a vampire. In his *Historia Rerum Anglicarum* William of Newburgh, the chronicler who lived around 1135 to 1200, described how a deceased master of the castle – 'a stranger to God's grace and whose crimes were many' – would rise from his tomb during the hours of darkness to prowl the streets of the sleeping town.

The local priest told the historian how his body left such a stench of death and corruption behind him that pestilence broke out. Many townsfolk fled to escape the fate overtaking so many of their neighbours. A number of men, blaming the vampire for the plague, banded together to rid themselves of the menace.

Alnwick Castle.

In Newburgh Priory William wrote:

> They armed themselves, therefore, with sharp spades and betaking themselves to the cemetery, they began to dig. And whilst they yet thought they would have to dig much deeper, they came upon the body covered with but a thin layer of earth. It was gorged and swollen with a frightful corpulence ...

One of the men struck the bloated body with the edge of his spade and from the wound came a gush of fresh blood, proving that it was indeed the vampire. Immediately the corpse of the erstwhile master of the castle was taken beyond the precincts of Alnwick and burned to ashes. After this the pestilence subsided.

Visiting Information

Situated in the town of Alnwick, Northumberland. Open daily 1 April to 30 October.

ARUNDEL CASTLE

Arundel Castle, the home of the Dukes of Norfolk and their ancestors for seven centuries, has often been described as Windsor Castle on a smaller scale. It is complete with a round keep, upper and lower baileys and stone steps protected by battlemented walls leading up to the keep. And like Windsor Castle it has its ghosts.

The building of the castle began during the reign of Edward the Confessor on the high ground above the River Arun, although it was not until William I gave the fortress to his relative, Roger Montgomery, that stone began to replace its timber construction.

One of Roger's sons, Earl Robert, rebelled against Henry I who besieged the castle in 1102. The fact that it was able to hold out for twelve weeks against a royal army indicated its strength.

When Henry I died, his queen, Adela of Louvain, retired to the castle where she fell in love with its lord, William d'Albini. He was a supporter of the Empress Matilda in her war with King Stephen in the chaotic years when, as a chronicler graphically put it, 'Christ and his saints slept.'

William d'Albini was known as 'William of the Strong Hand', and his nickname together with the lion rampant on the Albini arms is said to have originated when he was in Paris contending in a tournament. He performed so well in the lists that the Dowager Queen of France made it clear that she would not be averse to him as a husband. He made it equally clear that he was already betrothed to the Dowager Queen of England.

Feeling insulted, the French queen tricked d'Albini into a grotto in her palace garden where a hungry lion was waiting. D'Albini rushed at the animal, wrenched its jaws apart and pulled out its tongue.

After returning to England and marrying Adela he became the Earl of Arundel. When the Empress Matilda arrived in England to claim the throne he allowed her to stay at Arundel Castle. King Stephen surrounded it with his army and soon had the empress in his power, but the king was too much of a gentleman for his own good. Many a monarch in those days would have seized the opportunity to remove his rival by a stroke of the headsman's axe, but Stephen merely gave her safe conduct to Bristol.

Arundel Castle.

She repaid this courtesy by joining with her half-brother, Earl Robert, against the king and soon became mistress of the West of England.

When her son, Henry II, became England's first Plantagenet king, William d'Albini was rewarded for his services by being given command of the king's army in Normandy, and it was during this period that the Arundel's round keep was built on the motte within the castle walls.

In the Civil War, Parliamentarian forces besieged Arundel for eighteen days, bombarding with a canon placed in the tower of nearby St Nicholas's church. The marks left by the cannonballs are still to be seen on the walls of the barbican towers.

Cromwell's artillery sounded the death knell for castles as places of military importance, and Arundel was left a ruin until 1716, when the 8th Duke of Norfolk began to restore it. This work was carried on by his descendants until today Arundel stands in its former glory.

As one would expect from such a historical background, the castle has its fair share of ghosts. These include the silvery shape of a young girl sometimes seen in the moonlight near one of the towers. It is believed that she threw herself from it as the result of an unhappy love affair.

Another ghost, the Blue Man, has appeared in the library bending over an ancient book. Dressed in a blue garb dating from the time of Charles II, he seems to be seeking some piece of information which he fails to find.

In the castle kitchen during the dead of night there is sometimes heard the rattle of pots and pans, the sound of a scullion hard at work. It is a supernatural echo going back two centuries when a kitchen lad was brutally ill-treated there.

From time to time, a more impressive sound echoes from the past: the noise of the Parliamentarian artillery which pounded the castle walls during the Christmas siege of 1643.

It is an old Arundel legend that when one of the family is about to die, a mysterious white bird is observed fluttering desperately against the panes of one of the castle windows.

Visiting Information

Situated in the centre of Arundel, Sussex. Open 31 March to 4 November, Tuesday to Sunday.

BAMBURGH CASTLE

As befits a castle with a tradition of once being Sir Lancelot's 'Joyous Garde', Bamburgh Castle is haunted by a knight who appears in the massive twelfth-century keep. The castle is an apt setting for such a phantom. Looming majestically over stretches of pale golden sands and dunes, it has a storybook atmosphere, heightened by the restoration work commissioned by the 1st Lord Armstrong of the Vickers Armstrong Company.

The castle has witnessed the spectrum of English history – the setting up of Aidan's monastery on nearby Lindisfarne, raids by the Vikings in the ninth century and rebellion against William II, the hated Red King.

Its lord during the rebellion was Robert de Mowbray, Earl of Northumberland, who was captured in the fighting when the castle was besieged by royal troops. King William II took the fettered earl within sight of the battlements and sent a message to the earl's lady, who still held the castle, that unless the gates were opened she would see her husband's eyes gouged out. Bamburgh surrendered.

The Scots also besieged the castle during the unhappy reign of King Stephen, breaching a wall and slaying a hundred of the garrison. During the reign of King John the castellan had a profitable sideline in piracy, preying on coastal vessels.

It was besieged again by Yorkists during the Wars of the Roses when a new weapon was eroding the supremacy of the castles – the cannon.

In the siege of 1464, Edward IV was so sorry to see artillery used on such a fine fortress that he warned the Lancastrian defenders that for every shot fired one of them would pay with his head when it fell. Later Bamburgh became the first British castle to surrender to the power of gunpowder. After this the castle was allowed to deteriorate, and at the beginning of the eighteenth century it passed into the hands of the Crewe family, one of whom was Thomas Forster, who became the famous 'Pretender's General' in the Jacobite Rebellion of 1715.

Soon afterwards it was handed over to a charity run by Dr John Sharp, the curate of the village of Bamburgh, who, after having seen so many ships wrecked off the treacherous coast, started a lifeboat service. Thus the castle became Britain's first lifeboat station. The

Bamburgh Castle.

most spectacular rescue to take place near here happened in 1838, when Grace Darling and her father rowed through a gale from their lighthouse on the nearby Farne Islands to rescue survivors from the wrecked steamship *Forfarshire*.

It is not known to which period in the castle's colourful story its ghost goes back to. When he has been seen, his figure has been described as grey and indistinct but the fact that he is wearing armour is apparent from the clank of steel and the metallic sound of his footsteps. He is, in fact, a clanking ghost.

If visiting Bamburgh Castle it is worth spending a little time at the Grace Darling Museum in the town.

Visiting Information

The castle overlooks the sea, close to the village of Bamburgh, Northumberland. Open daily from 11 February to 31 October, weekends 1 November to 15 February.

BERRY POMEROY CASTLE

Ruined Berry Pomeroy Castle, dating back to the Norman Conquest, is noted for its ghosts. The least horrific are a pair of lovers who have been glimpsed vainly trying to touch each other with phantom hands above the gatehouse arch. Long ago the baron's daughter fell in love with a member of a family with whom the Pomeroys had a deadly feud. This Romeo and Juliet situation ended when the girl's brother slew them both for the honour of the family.

The history of the castle goes back to the Norman Conquest when it was built by Ralph Pomerai who was one of the adventurers who crossed the Channel with William the Conqueror. The lurid events in the castle's story are illustrated by one of his descendants, Henry de Pomerai. When Richard Coeur de Lion was away on a crusade Henry sided with Prince John, who was intriguing against the king. When Richard returned from the Holy Land he had doubts about Henry's loyalty. He therefore sent a herald to Berry Pomeroy to report on Henry's real allegiance. When the herald had gathered evidence against Henry the king challenged Henry to appear before the High Court on a treason charge.

Henry's answer was to kill the herald with a dagger and flee to Cornwall, where he took over the castle on St Michael's Mount. Here he was besieged by forces under the command of the Archbishop of Canterbury. When he could no longer hold out against them he committed suicide in the Roman fashion by having his veins opened by a surgeon. It is not known if his spirit ever returned to Berry Pomeroy to become one of the castle's ghostly community.

The castle's best-known story tells of two sisters, Margaret and Eleanor Pomeroy, who fell in love with the same man. Lady Eleanor, the elder of the two and mistress of the castle, locked her sister in a dungeon, now known as St Margaret's Tower. Here she starved to death after a long imprisonment.

Eleanor may have won the man she desired but her crime was never forgotten as Margaret's tormented spectre returns as a reminder of the murder. According to a pamphlet on Berry Pomeroy Castle by S.M. Ellis: 'Now on certain nights of the year, the lovely Margaret is said to arise from her entombed dungeon, leaving St Margaret's

Berry Pomeroy Castle.

Tower and walk along the ramparts in long white flowing robes and beckon to the beholder to come and join her in the dungeon below.'

Another unhappy ghost is known as the Blue Lady who, wearing a blue hooded cape, searches the castle grounds for her baby. She is said to have had an incestuous relationship with her father, one of the lords of the castle. When his daughter gave birth to his child he strangled it with his own hands. Another version of the legend suggests the girl smothered the infant herself.

An account of this haunting was written by Sir Walter Farquhar whose dedication to medicine was rewarded with a baronetcy in 1796. Called to Berry Pomeroy, where the wife of the caretaker was dangerously ill, he was asked to wait in a dark but handsomely furnished room. After a few minutes a young woman in blue appeared silently. Ignoring the doctor she ascended a flight of stairs where light from a window caught her features before she moved from sight. Afterwards Sir Walter wrote: 'If ever human face exhibited agony and remorse ... if ever features betrayed within the wearer's bosom there dwelt a hell, those features were then presented to me.'

The doctor forgot the strange figure when tending his ailing patient but next day, his patient rallied and he inquired about the mysterious woman.

'My poor wife! That it should come to this!' cried the caretaker and then explained, 'You have seen the ghost of the daughter of a former baron who bore a child to her own father. In that room the fruit of their incestuous intercourse was strangled by the guilty mother. Now, whenever death is about to come to the castle the crazed phantom is seen at the scene of the crime. When my son was drowned she came – now it is my wife!'

'Your wife is better,' said the doctor. 'It is absurd to talk about omens.' But, according to his testimony, the caretaker's wife died an hour later.

An unusual aspect of this castle's hauntings is that its phantoms have been seen in daylight.

Visiting Information

Situated close to Berry Pomeroy village, north of Totnes, Devon. The ruin is open to visit.

BRAMBER CASTLE

The most pathetic phantoms connected with an English castle are those of the starving children who haunt the road which runs through the Sussex village of Bramber. Dominating the village is the tower-like ruin of the castle which was built at the close of the eleventh century on a natural mound above the River Adur by William de Braose. It is the ghosts of his children who have been glimpsed gazing at the ruin of their home, or running hand-in-hand through the village.

Their tragedy began when King John, suspecting their father of disloyalty, decided to take his four children as hostages, a not uncommon practice in those unsettled times.

Bramber Castle.

In the eighteenth century the historian Francis Grosse wrote:

> In the year 1208 King John, suspecting divers of the nobility sent to demand hostages for their fidelity, among the rest to William de Braose of whom his messengers demanded his children which Matilda his wife, according to Matthew Paris, gave this answer that she could not trust her children with the King who had so basely murdered his own nephew, Prince Arthur, whom he was in honour bound to protect. This speech being reported to the King, he was greatly insensed thereto and secretly sent soldiers to seize the whole family. But they receiving private information of his intent fled to Ireland, where he [King John] in the year 1210, making them prisoners sent them to England and, closely confining them in Windsor Castle, he caused them to be starved to death. Some say William escaped to France where he shortly died.

Although Bramber Castle was mostly destroyed in the Civil War, the spectres of King John's young victims have been seen by its ruins. They hold out their hands as though begging for food but they fade away the moment they are spoken to.

Visiting Information

Situated in the village of Bramber, Sussex.

CAERPHILLY CASTLE

Among the castles that have harbingers of doom is Caerphilly Castle which was plagued by a hag-like apparition known in folklore as the Gwrach-y-rhibyn. When the de Clare family were owners of the castle its appearance heralded doom for the castellan.

Now an impressive ruin, it is one of the largest castles in Britain and was originally a Roman fort. Its medieval fortifications were begun in 1268 by Gilbert de Clare, Earl of Gloucester and Lord of Glamorgan. Its most unusual feature is a shattered tower that leans at a seemingly impossible angle. There are several traditional tales as to how it came about.

The most dramatic is that when the castle was being besieged by Queen Isabella's forces in 1326 the defenders beat back attacks by pouring molten lead on the enemy from the battlements of the tower. In the end the queen's troops managed to capture the castle, after which they allowed the water of the moat to flow into the cellar where furnaces heated the cauldrons of lead. The result was a steam explosion which tore the tower apart.

Even after the de Clares left and the castle fell into disrepair, the Gwrach-y-rhibyn still appeared there when a descendant of the family was on the point of death. The ill-omened harpy always rose from a piece of swampy ground near the great moat, and from here she glided towards the castle ruins where she vanished.

Visiting Information

Situated at Caerphilly, Glamorgan. Open daily.

CAISTER CASTLE

O f the castles that are haunted by supernatural harbingers of disaster, Caister Castle had one of the most spectacular.

One of England's first castles to be constructed of brick, it was built in 1435 by Sir John Fastolf whose name and nature were adapted by William Shakespeare into one of his best-known characters. A highly successful soldier, Sir John built the castle with money raised by ransoming a French knight he had captured when campaigning in France with Henry V. It was also Sir John's idea to protect Caister Castle by elaborate water defences. Caister's ghostly portent goes back to that time.

The owners of the castle feared that death was close to a member of the family when a phantom coach, unpleasantly like a horse-drawn hearse, swayed up to the castle as fast as the headless driver could urge his spectral horses. After passing through the gates as though they were not there, it would circle the courtyard several times before vanishing in the direction from which it had appeared.

It is a mystery as to why such a sinister phenomenon should be in the form of a coach but with ghost-lore mystery is commonplace.

When the Paston family – the authors of the famous *Paston Letters* – inherited the castle in 1459 they also inherited the prophetic coach. Ten years later, after the Wars of the Roses had broken out, the castle was attacked by a large army commanded by the Duke of Norfolk. The castle had only thirty men to defend it and in fear Margaret Paston wrote to a son in London: 'Your brother and his fellowship stand in great jeopardy at Caister ... Daubeney and Berney be dead and divers others be greatly hurt, and they fail gun-powder and arrows and the place is sore broken by guns.'

Yet even though the Pastons were greatly outnumbered reinforcements had to be brought up before Caister finally fell.

When Norfolk died seven years later the Pastons re-occupied the castle, and once more the sinister coach would appear before a family death.

Caister Castle.

Visiting Information

The castle stands close to Caister-on-Sea, Norfolk. Open, apart from Saturdays, from the middle of May to the last Friday in September.

CARLISLE CASTLE

A mysterious phantom has been seen in Carlisle Castle, on one occasion with tragic consequences.

William Rufus, the son of William the Conqueror, began the construction of the castle in 1092 and additions continued through the Middle Ages. At one stage in its eventful history it was the home of Andrew Harcla, Earl of Carlisle, who was executed on account of his alliance with Robert the Bruce.

Mary Queen of Scots began her long years of imprisonment here, and during the Civil War Sir Thomas Glenham held it for the king and only surrendered to a Scots army when its besieged garrison were trying to survive on 'rats, linseed meal and dogs'.

In 1745 it fell to the Jacobites who sent the news that they had captured a hundred barrels of gunpowder to Prince Charles Edward – Bonnie Prince Charlie – who was staying at Brampton, a small town to the east of Carlisle.

After the defeat of the rebels at Culloden, many pro-Stewart Scots were imprisoned here; their cells are still to be seen. Many alterations were made to the castle in the decade prior to 1835, when a parade ground and barracks were built. It was during the demolition and reconstruction that the skeleton of a lady was discovered bricked into the wall of the second storey of the keep. She was dressed in silk tartan, there were valuable rings on her fingers and her feet rested on silk kerchiefs. No one could guess her identity or why her body was sealed in, though there was great speculation as to whether she had been walled up alive.

It was probably her phantom which had been seen by a soldier of the 93rd Regiment stationed at the castle in 1842. One night he was on guard duty in the precincts of the keep when he challenged a figure approaching through the darkness. When he received no reply the sentry advanced towards it, shouting to rouse the guard as he did so. When he reached the figure it faded in front of his eyes and he collapsed with shock. He was found unconscious with his bayonet still embedded in the wall from an ineffectual lunge at the mysterious intruder. He recovered long enough to tell of the apparition but he died several hours later.

Carlisle Castle.

Visiting Information

Situated close to the centre of Carlisle, Cumbria. Open daily.

CASTELL COCH

Although Castell Coch is a romantic pseudo-gothic castle that only goes back to Victorian times it has a centuries-old ghost. The present castle was built by the Marquis of Bute on the foundations of a thirteenth-century fortress once held by the famed warrior Ifor Bach. The ghost it inherited from the old castle is that of a cavalier who, according to local folklore, is searching for a golden hoard hidden in a subterranean chamber centuries ago by Ifor Bach.

There is a hint of the Arthurian legend in such a tale because as well as a treasure there is a sleeping army of Ifor's men waiting to be re-animated on their master's return. It is similar to the Arthurian legend of sleeping knights waiting to be awakened.

The folktale adds that the treasure is guarded by three terrible eagles that tear to shreds men foolish enough to enter the mysterious vault.

A cavalier, perhaps hoping to find gold to help finance the royalist cause, thought he would outwit the guardians by wearing armour which had been given a holy blessing. It proved to be ineffectual when he lost his life in the quest. Since then his spectre has returned to the ancient site.

It is a quaint old tale, but there may just be some truth in it. After all, Heinrich Schliemann found the ruins of Troy from clues in Homer's *Iliad* which until then had been regarded as an ancient work of imagination.

Visiting Information

Situated off the A470, the castle is close to the village of Tongwynlais, Glamorgan, 5 miles north of Cardiff. Open daily.

CASTLE RISING

The story of the royal ghost at Castle Rising goes back seven centuries and involves Nottingham Castle as well. When Edward II was overthrown by his queen Isabella, the 'She Wolf of France', and her lover Roger Mortimer, Parliament offered the crown of England to King Edward's son, also called Edward. He was fifteen at the time and he refused to accept it unless his imprisoned father officially abdicated.

When the captive monarch renounced the throne young Edward was crowned Edward III in January 1327 but he was a sovereign in name only. The real power remained in the hands of his mother, Queen Isabella, and Roger Mortimer who had been created Earl of March. The couple in effect ruled England and in 1330 they were staying at Nottingham Castle where they were guarded by Mortimer's Welsh archers against popular detestation.

In that year Edward III, then seventeen, determined to stop being a puppet and avenge his father who had been murdered in Berkeley Castle, little doubt on the command of Mortimer.

The royal castellan told the young king of a secret tunnel which led into the precincts of the castle from an inn called the Trip to Jerusalem. The inn, which claims to be the oldest in England, is partly excavated from the cliff beneath the castle. The curious name came when crusaders congregated there before travelling to the Holy Land, the word *trypp* being the old English word for a halt.

At midnight on 19 October 1330 a number of the king's chosen companions came to the inn and crept up the secret tunnel into the castle, where they found Edward waiting for them outside his mother's door. They burst in and the king seized Mortimer, ignoring Isabella's plea '*Bel fitz, eiez pitie du gentil Mortimer*!' – in Norman French 'Fair son, have pity on the gentle Mortimer!'

According to tradition, Mortimer was held in a dungeon situated in the rock beneath the the castle and close to the inn. Later he was conveyed to London where he was charged with having usurped King Edward's authority and 'murdered and killed the King's father.' Judged guilty, he was the first prisoner to be hanged at Tyburn.

Castle Rising.

Tactfully no mention was made of his liaison with Queen Isabella, who was confined for the rest of her life as a prisoner in Castle Rising in Norfolk.

The haunting of the Trip to Jerusalem has been manifested by ghostly sounds which have echoed through the walls of the inn's subterranean chambers. They were not random sounds but, emanating from Mortimer's Hole, were regular as though some despairing captive was pacing up and down.

During the Second World War a group of American GIs left the Trip to Jerusalem late at night and walked past the castle walls. Suddenly they heard the disembodied voice of a woman screaming 'foreign words' in the air above them. When they recounted their experience to locals familiar with the lore of the castle they were told

The Trip to Jerusalem Inn.

that what they had heard was the ghostly voice of Queen Isabella crying, '*Bel fitz, eiez pitie du gentil Mortimer!*'

But it is at Castle Rising that Isabella's ghost has been most active. The castle, standing on the site of a Roman fort, had been built soon after the Norman Conquest, and while the queen was incarcerated there its lord was her grandson the Black Prince but this seems to have made no difference to her fate.

If the unearthly bursts of maniacal laughter, which have been heard resounding within the castle, are anything to go by, the queen lost her reason before her death. Her demented spectre has also been glimpsed hurrying wildly along the castle ramparts.

Visiting Information

Situated in the village of Castle Rising, 4½ miles from King's Lynn. Open daily from 1 April to 1 November. Wednesdays to Sundays only from 2 November to 31 March.

CAWOOD CASTLE

awood Castle was originally the palace of the Archbishop
of York, built on the site of King Athelstan's hall, and its
surviving gatehouse is now incorporated into a farm building.
Once it was haunted by a tragic female ghost who sought retribution
for a murder most foul. The circumstances were documented in
John Aubrey's *Miscellanies* which was published a short while after
the event.

The drama began on Palm Monday, 14 April 1690, when William
Barwick took his wife Mary, described as 'big with child', walking by
the walls of the castle. He had grown to resent her. Why, he never
explained at his trial, but the inference was that having got her
pregnant he was forced to marry her.

Overcome by a sudden rage, he seized his unfortunate wife and
pushed her into a deserted pond. He waited until the bubbles of the
drowning woman ceased to rise, then hid the body in a tangle of
weeds. An old account adds to the horror of the crime by stating that
Berwick 'had the cruelty to behold the motion of the infant yet warm
in her womb.'

The next night he returned to the castle and, taking a hay-spade
from a nearby rick, dug a shallow grave on the bank of the pond and
buried his victim.

Berwick then visited the house of his brother-in-law Thomas
Lofthouse and told him that Mary had gone to her uncle's house in
Selby where she would stay for her confinement. A description of
what followed was published in John Aubrey's *Miscellanies*:

Heaven would not be so deluded, but raised up the ghost of the
murdered woman to make the discovery. And therefore it was
upon Easter Tuesday following, about two of the clock in the
afternoon, the forementioned Lofthouse having occasion to water
a hedge not far from his house; as he was going for the second pail
full, an apparition went before him in the shape of a woman and
soon after sat down right upon a rising green grass-plat, right over
against the pond. He walked by her as he went to the pond; and
as he returned with the pail looking sideways to see whether she
remained in the same place, he found she did, and that she seemed

to dandle something on her lap that looked like a white bag (as he thought) which he had not observed before. So soon as he had emptied his pail, he went into his yard to see whether he could see her again but she had vanished.

Later he said that the woman wore a white hood such as one his wife usually wore and that she looked like his wife's sister, the wife of William Berwick.

For the rest of the day Lofthouse was worried by what he had seen and finally told his wife he believed he had seen a ghost. Mrs Lofthouse feared that her sister had been a victim of foul play and told her husband to search for her. He recalled how Berwick had told him his wife was going to her uncle's house, and he went straight to Selby. There he learned that no one had seen Mr and Mrs Berwick and he became more and more suspicious of his brother-in-law. He went to the Lord Mayor of York with his suspicions and William Berwick was arrested.

On 16 September he pleaded not guilty at the York Assizes, and denied a confession he had made earlier. Part of the disputed confession read that he drowned his wife in a pond 'and upon the bank of the said pond, did bury her and further that he was within sight of Cawood Castle'.

After Thomas Lofthouse's evidence had been heard – in which he described how he had seen the ghost – and the court heard how the body had been found by the pond in clothing like Lofthouse had seen on the apparition, William Barwick was sentenced to death, duly executed and his body was left hanging in chains as a dreadful example.

Visiting Information

Situated in the village of Cawood, Yorkshire, north-west of Selby. Holiday visits can be arranged.

CLAYPOTTS CASTLE

It is a White Lady who is believed to appear at a high window in Dundee's Claypotts Castle each 29 May, waving a white handkerchief almost as though it was a signal of distress. Her story goes back to Cardinal Beaton, who lived from 1494 to 1546 and became notorious in Scottish history for his persecution of Protestants.

Despite the office he held in the Church, Beaton had two sons and a daughter by his mistress Marion Ogilvy who, according to many accounts, became the White Lady of Claypotts.

An unreliable tradition claims that the cardinal actually built the castle for her, and she used to signal to him with her handkerchief when he was at his Castle of St Andrews across the Tay.

The actual dating of the legend is speculative as it is thought that Claypotts was built in 1569, which would be twenty-three years after the cardinal had been assassinated. One theory is that Marion Ogilvy could have waved from an earlier building on the site.

There is a tendency throughout the years for ghosts to be given convenient historical names and neat explanations. In this case the accepted tradition regarding the Claypotts phantom is that she was signalling to the cardinal on 29 May when news came of his violent death.

Whether the lady who annually waves from Claypotts was Beaton's mistress or not is open to question, but there have been so many reports of the phenomenon that if it is not her it must be some other equally distressed lady.

Visiting Information

Situated in Dundee, Tayside. External viewing only.

CLOSEBURN CASTLE

A not uncommon tradition in British ghostlore is that of the supernatural harbinger – the phantom that presages ill fortune or death for families connected with certain castles. Such precursors of tragedy often have their origins lost in antiquity, but a few – such as the White Swan of Closeburn – have factual backgrounds.

For generations the Kirkpatrick family used Closeburn Castle. In the castle domain was a small lake and each summer two swans would arrive and remain there until autumn.

Year after year they returned to Closeburn, and their coming was eagerly expected by members of the family as they began regarding the two graceful birds as good luck symbols. This belief probably began when the wife of the lord of Closeburn was dangerously ill, then miraculously recovered her health just as the swans arrived.

The idea was emphasised when the young heir of the castle was close to death and his recovery coincided with the sight of the birds returning to the lake. Popular superstition credited the pair for living over a hundred years, but it is more likely that the Closeburn swans were several generations of birds. Nevertheless, they were a living tradition of the castle.

Tragedy came to these special waterfowl in the form of Robert Kirkpatrick, the thirteen-year-old heir of Closeburn. He had been taken to Edinburgh where he saw *The Merchant of Venice* and was very impressed when Bassanio regards the three caskets before choosing the one of lead.

He says, 'But let me to my fortune and the caskets,' he says. Portia replies, 'Let music sound while he doth make his choice. Then, if he lose, he makes a swan-like end ...' What intrigued Robert was not whether Bassanio would choose the right box and win Portia but the belief that swans suddenly found voice at their deaths hence the expression 'swansong'.

A keen young huntsman he determined to put the myth to the test. Soon afterwards he was walking by the lake with his bow and saw one of the swans sailing towards him over the water, no doubt expecting the customary tidbit. Instead it received an arrow in its breast.

The bird died without breaking into a swan song, and Robert felt a chill strike his heart as he realised the enormity of his cruel action. He knew how severely he would be punished if his father discovered that he had killed one of the birds that had long been mascots of the castle.

He waded into the water, seized the dead swan and dragged it into a patch of reeds where he hid until he could bury it out of sight of the castle.

Lamenting its mate, the surviving swan flew away, and Robert shivered as he heard his parents discussing the unusually early departure of the birds.

Next summer the inhabitants of the castle awaited the arrival of the swans, but no swan came that year nor for several years. Then one day at the end of spring a single swan landed on the lake, and those who saw it were struck by the curious blood-coloured mark on its breast feathers.

Several days passed, and the single swan was watched with anxiety, especially by Robert. There was something ominous about the bird as it glided up and down the lake. After a week the lord of Closeburn died unexpectedly, and the mourners noted that almost as soon as the breath left his body there was the beat of wings as the swan departed.

Years passed before the bird with the red feathers returned, and then it was found that at the same time a member of the Kirkpatrick family was drowning in a shipwreck. When news arrived of his death the ill-omened swan flew away to some unknown destination. From then on it only returned when one of the Kirkpatricks was about to die.

The last time this occurrence was recorded was on the wedding day of the widowed Sir Thomas Kirkpatrick who was the family's first baronet. His son Robert left the celebrations to stroll in the cool by the lake. Suddenly he saw a swan swimming towards him, a red mark standing out vividly in contrast to its white breast feathers.

Robert shuddered. It was as though the sight of the bird had sapped all the good humour of the occasion. When he returned to the castle his father made joking reference to his gloomy countenance. Roger explained about the eerie feeling the sight of the swan had induced. Sir Thomas tried to laugh him out of his odd mood and suggested that it might have resulted from too much wine. The young man nodded and retired to his room. By midnight he was dead.

The castle passed out of the hands of the family towards the eighteenth century, and since then the red-breasted swan has not returned.

Visiting Information

The castle stands near the village of Closeburn, Dumfries and Galloway, on private land.

CORFE CASTLE

The ghostly episode in the castle's history began in 975 when King Edward, later known as The Martyr, ascended the throne on the death of his father King Edgar. The late king had taken a second wife named Elfrida and by her had another son named Ethelred. Queen Elfrida tried to secure the succession for her own son but her attempt failed. Edward was duly crowned and was soon beloved by his subjects.

The queen then lived in retirement at Corfe Castle, which had been her royal husband's residence.

The castle goes back to Norman times, when William the Conqueror built a wooden tower on a motte which was transformed to a stone keep by Henry I. During the Civil War, the owner went to join the Royalist forces and left the castle in the charge of his wife, Lady Mary Banks. She successfully defended it when sieged by Parliamentary forces. During the final attack in 1646 an officer of the castle betrayed it in return for a promise of protection. Lady Mary and her children were give a safe conduct from the vanquished castle.

Later a vengeful Cromwell ordered it to be destroyed by gunpowder and so it remains a renowned ruin today.

The supernatural episode goes back to a day in March, 978, when young King Edward was hunting near Corfe and decided to pay his stepmother a courtesy call. As the hunting party had separated while chasing a deer, Edward was alone when he approached the twin towers of the castle gate, now known as the Martyr's Gate. A sentry recognised him and sent word to the queen so she could greet her royal stepson in the traditional manner.

Three servants were sent to the gate before the king could enter. One grasped the bridle of his horse, another handed him the customary welcoming wine cup and the third seized his free hand and made as though to kiss it. A moment later a dagger was plunged into his back, his horse bolted until it reached a brook at the bottom of the hill and its rider fell dead from the saddle.

After the disappearance of the king, Ethelred ascended the throne as his mother had planned.

Now the supernatural element enters the story. Local people noticed that a mysterious ray of ghostly light appeared above a well

The Martyr's Gate.

Corfe Castle.

near the castle. Finally the well was searched and the body of the murdered king was found and interred at the church of St Mary of Wareham.

Soon the well in which the body had been hidden gained miraculous healing properties and was named St Edward's Fountain.

Following this an old woman came forth with an amazing story. Before the assassins took Edward's body to the well they hid it under a covering in her hut, confident she could never witness against them as she was blind. Then one night the hut was filled with an aura of holy light. The woman saw this because suddenly her sight was miraculously restored.

As a result of these manifestations, and the exemplary nature of his short life, Edward was canonised by the Pope.

Visiting Information

The ruins stand close to Corfe Castle village, Dorset. Open all year apart from 25–26 December and a day in March – check website for details.

CORGARFF CASTLE

The savagery of clan feuds can be gauged by the pitiful state of ghosts whose lives ended in them. Corgarff Castle, which guards the entrance to the Lecht Pass in Aberdeenshire, has had supernatural reminders of such tragic conflicts.

Built in 1537, the castle was used by Thomas Erskine, Earl of Mar. A hundred years earlier the Crown annexed lands belonging to the earldom but at the beginning of the sixteenth century King James IV of Scotland granted them to the 1st Lord Elphinstone. Later through his grandson's marriage Corgarff was passed on to the Forbes family.

There was a long-standing feud between the Forbeses and the Gordon clan. In November 1571 Adam Gordon, laird of Auchindoun Castle decided to capture Corgarff while its master was away. When he and his followers arrived at the castle Margaret, the wife of the absent lord, stood up to them and refused to give up her home.

In the assault that followed Margaret was burned alive after the attackers prevented her and her family and servants from escaping when part of the castle was set on fire.

The wraiths of those twenty-seven unfortunates who perished in the flames long haunted the castle. After further vicissitudes, which included being burnt again by the Jacobites, its ruined tower was restored in the 1960s. It is now in the care of the Department of the Environment.

Visiting Information

Situated close to the village of Corgarff, Aberdeenshire. Open daily April to September, Saturdays and Sundays only October to March.

CORTACHY CASTLE

A particular British form of haunting is that of the Phantom Drummer. One of the most famous of these psychical cases concerned the Drummer of Tedworth. During the seventeenth century the supernatural beating of a drum – confiscated from an itinerant drummer who had demanded money with menaces – plagued the household of John Monpesson, a local magistrate, for over two years.

The mysterious drumming, which began in March 1661, was so spectacular that a Royal Commission was set up to investigate it by command of Charles II.

At least three castles have echoed with similar unearthly tattoos, the foremost being Scotland's Cortachy Castle where the beat of a long-dead drummer portended death for members of the Airlie family which resided there from 1625.

There are several treasured heirlooms in the castle which indicate the character and allegiances of the Airlies. They include a prayer book left behind by the fugitive Charles II when he stayed at the castle having escaped from the Covenanters, and there is a silver drinking cup and a sword carried by Lord Ogilvy, a son to the 3rd Earl of Airlie, at Culloden.

There are also the remains of an ancient drum which legend tells was once played by the drummer who haunts the castle.

Three versions of the story behind the ill-omened drumming have been handed down though the generations. One is that a drummer boy, taken prisoner in a clan feud with the Campbells, was held at Airlie Castle (which had been the previous seat of the family) and while there died when the castle was burnt down in the reign of Charles I. The boy's posthumous resentment then followed James, Lord Ogilvy, when he moved to Cortachy and became the 1st Earl of Airlie.

Another version is that the drummer was a herald from the Lindsay Clan who were frequently in conflict with the Lords of Airlie. The arrogant message he delivered after playing a roll on his instrument so enraged the Earl of Airlie that he had the unfortunate lad seized and hurled from the top of the castle wall.

The most popular account of the tragedy, however, is that a good-looking young drummer in service of the earl was discovered having an affair with the lady of the castle. The cuckolded husband ordered his guards to squeeze the reckless lover into his drum and roll it out of the window of the highest turret. The drummer did not die instantly. When the earl went to the base of the wall to see the result of his command, the victim managed to gasp a curse before he expired, declaring his ghost would haunt the earl's descendants as long as they held the castle.

Whatever the true story behind the unfortunate drummer, there was no shortage of belief that he returned from beyond the grave to fulfil the curse.

The most complete description of the drumming was published in Catherine Crowe's famous *The Night Side of Nature*, one of the early books on the supernatural. The author described how in 1845 a certain Miss Margaret Dalrymple, accompanied by her maid Mrs Ann Day, heard the beating of a drum under her window while dressing for dinner on the first night of a visit to Cortachy. During the dinner she turned to Lord Airlie and asked, 'My Lord, who is your drummer?'

At the question the earl paled while his wife and several of the dinner party looked embarrassed. After the dinner she took the opportunity to speak to a member of the family and say she had not wished to cause any unpleasantness by her unwitting remark but was quite mystified by its effect.

She was told the story of the phantom drummer and how the last time he was heard was shortly before the death of the previous countess, the earl's former wife, which explained why his lordship became so pale.

Miss Dalrymple resolved to say nothing more about the drumming but next morning her maid heard the beating of a drum. At first it sounded as though it was in the courtyard, then seemed to echo in the house as though approaching the turret in which she and her mistress were lodged and continued outside the door. But there was no flesh-and-blood drummer there.

The next day Miss Dalrymple had the same experience as her maid and was so alarmed by it that she cut short her stay. According to Mrs Crowe the death of the countess 'sadly verified the prognostic'.

She wrote: 'I have heard that a paper was found in her desk after her death declaring her conviction that the drum was for her.'

Visiting Information

Situated 3½ miles north of Kirriemuir, Angus. Open for walks in the gardens. Check for details with the estate office.

CRATHES CASTLE

Often described as a 'fairytale castle' Crathes has an aptly named Green Lady's Room. The castle, which was built in 1553, has many treasures, one of the most historic being the Horn of Leys, a jewelled ivory horn which Robert the Bruce gave to the Burnett family who owned the castle until 1966 when Sir James Burnett presented it to the National Trust of Scotland.

The castle ghost, known as the Green Lady of Crathes, has been known to glide across the room that is named after her, usually before a death occurred in the Burnett family. Each time she appeared she

Crathes Castle.

would cross the room to an ancient carved fireplace where she would lift up a child, after which she would fade away.

When renovations were being carried out, workmen unearthed the skeletons of a woman and a baby which were thought to have been the mortal remains of the phantoms.

Visiting Information

Situated close to Crathes village, a short distance east of Banchory, Aberdeenshire. Open daily April to October, Saturdays only November to March.

CULZEAN CASTLE

It is the sound of bagpipes once played by a Kennedy piper that haunts Culzean Castle. Today the castle is a collection of Georgian buildings – described as '18th century Picturesque' – surrounding an ancient tower which was once the stronghold of the Kennedy Clan.

In the sixteenth century the family divided and actually fought a battle, the Kennedys of Culzean becoming the victors. It is not know whether the phantom piper goes back to that time. There is no explanatory legend but it has not been unusual, when the wind howls from the Firth of Clyde, for the mysterious lament of his pipes to have been heard above the gale.

Visiting Information

Overlooking the Firth of Clyde, the castle stands 4 miles west of Maybole, Ayrshire. Open daily April to October.

Culzean Castle.

DACRE CASTLE

Dacre Castle has a royal haunting that goes back hundreds of years. The castle is really a pele tower, built in the thirteenth century by Ranulph Dacre on the earthworks of an earlier fortification. Parts of its moat are still to be seen, and one of its rooms is still known as the Kings' Room, doubtless commemorating an historic meeting of three kings that took place there long ago.

King Athelstan had given his sister in marriage to Sithric, King of Northumbria, but the latter failed to meet his obligations to the Saxon monarch. He died before retribution could catch up with him but his two sons, Anlaf and Guthred, were forced to flee to the court of King Constantine of Scotland. He attempted to regain Northumbria for the brothers with the aid of King Donal of Strathclyde, but their campaign failed and finally the two northern kings met Athelstan at the site of Dacre Castle.

The meeting was barely over when the kingdoms of the north decided to humble the Saxon king, and to this end they were joined by the Kings of Cumbria, Wales, Ireland, and the Danes who sailed into the Humber in a great fleet of ships to occupy Northumbria.

It seemed the Saxons would be overwhelmed by the confederation of Celts and Danes which faced them on the field of Brunnanburgh. But, led by King Athelstan and his brother Edmund, the Saxons attacked the invading army with such valour that they won the day.

Some lines in the *Anglo-Saxon Chronicle* give us an inkling of this Dark Age victory:

> Then the Norsemen departed in their nailed ships, bloodstained survivors of spears, on Dingsmere over the the deep water to seek Dublin, Ireland, once more, sorry of heart. The two brothers likewise, king and atheling both, sought their own country, the land of the West Saxons, exulting in war. They left behind them, to joy in the carrion, the black and horn-beaked raven with his dusky plumage, and the dun-feathered eagle with his white-tipped tail, greedy hawk of battle, to take toll of the corpses...

Why the shades of the three kings who met before this bloody conflict should continue to return to Dacre Castle none can say, but – though

Dacre Castle.

the ages have passed since the ravens fed on their dead followers – their phantoms have appeared in the grounds about the castle.

Visiting Information

Situated at Dacre village, close to Penrith, Cumbria, the castle is on private land.

DILSTON CASTLE

It is the ghost of Lady Derwentwater who haunts the ruins of Dilston Hall, waiting for her lord who will never return. Sometimes her lamp, as spectral as herself, shines as a beacon from a high paneless window where, in happier days, she used to watch for his coming.

There is doubt as to when the original castle was built, but the tomb in Hexham Abbey of one of its former lords Sir Thomas de Devilstone, is dated 1297. The present rectangular tower, built close to the bank of a stream known as Devil's Water, dates back to the fifteenth century when the property passed into the hands of Sir Edward Radcliffe. His descendants, always loyal to the Stewart cause, temporarily lost their possessions during the Commonwealth.

With the Restoration the family regained their land and James II gave Francis Radcliffe the titles of Baron Dilston, Viscount Langley and Earl of Derwentwater. It is his grandson, James, the 3rd Earl of Derwentwater, who concerns us. He succeeded the title in 1705 at the age of seventeen, having been educated at the court of St Germain with the son of the exiled King James following the Glorious Revolution of 1688. His mother was Lady Mary, the daughter of Charles II by Moll Davis.

As young Lord Derwentwater James proved to be very popular throughout the district. A Border ballad of the time described him thus:

> O, Derwentwater's a bonnie lord,
> And golden is his hair,
> And glinting is his hawking eye,
> Wi' kind love dwelling there.

In 1712 James married a Catholic lady named Anna Webb. Three years later, the name of the young earl was among those of several northern gentlemen against whom warrants were issued on account of their Jacobite sympathies. James and his retainers joined the rebels seeking to replace George I, who had come from Hanover the year before.

He was among the seven rebel lords captured and imprisoned in the Tower of London. He pleaded guilty when charged with treason at Westminster Hall and threw himself on the king's mercy. However,

King George had no mercy and Lord Derwentwater was beheaded at Tower Hill on 24 February 1716. Strange signs accompanied the execution: blood dripped from the spouts of Dilston Castle, corn from the local mill was stained a reddish hue, as was the Devil's Water, which from that day ceased to be a prattling stream and took on a sombre appearance.

An old account states:

> Tis said that the instant the noble head was severed from his body, a strange moaning sound of agonised sorrow was uttered by the vast multitude of spectators, and far and wide across the northern counties bitter tears were shed and expressions of horror and grief uttered for the hapless fate of the winsome young earl.

It took two weeks for his body to be brought from London to the Chapel of St Mary Magdalene which stands close to the castle. As the procession bore the coffin on the last stage of its mournful journey to Dilston there was such an usually brilliant display of the Aurora Borealis that ever since have been referred to in the district as the Derwentwater Lights, and which afterwards have been said to appear on each anniversary of the earl's execution.

The local people's grief at the loss of their lord turned to anger against his wife Anna when a rumour spread that she had shamed him into joining the hapless revolution.

She decided to leave the castle and from then on moved from one place to another until she died in 1723 at the age of thirty. Although the threatening attitude of the locals had driven her away from her home, her spirit has been seen at Dilston with her lamp which she held as a guiding light when he was away with the Jacobites.

Visiting Information

Situated close to Dilston village west of Hexham, Northumberland. On private land.

DOVER CASTLE

It is appropriate that the ghost of Dover Castle has a military connection. The castle's strategic value has been recognised from pre-Roman times. Within its precincts are the 800ft-high remains of a Roman lighthouse. In turn the Normans recognised the importance of the site and built much of the castle which is to be seen today, surrounding it with two walls, the inner having fourteen towers and the outer twenty-seven. The inner bailey and huge keep was built by order of Henry II.

In 1216 the castle withstood a siege by the army of the French Dauphin, who had been invited to England by the barons who wanted to depose King John.

During the Civil War it fell to the Roundheads after a dozen of Cromwell's local supporters scaled the walls and talked the royal castellan into opening the castle gates. A Roundhead detachment had to make a forced march from Canterbury to secure their victory.

During the Napoleonic Wars the castle was regarded as a key defence point and over 200 cannons were installed there. It was at this time that a drummer boy was murdered within the castle walls, presumably by having his head cut off, for the ghost that haunts the castle with a drum is headless.

Visiting Information

The castle stands on the eastern side of Dover, Kent. Open at weekends.

DUNSTAFFNAGE CASTLE

Standing on a promontory overlooking Loch Linnhe, Dunstaffnage is steeped in history. It is haunted, not by a 'normal' ghost but a fairy woman known as a Glaistig or Elle Maid, a benign folklore entity in Scotland. Glaistigs were believed to associate themselves closely with the fortunes of the families they adopted, often uttering supernatural cries of joy or sorrow when good or ill fortune was about to befall them.

The castle was once the home of Scottish kings before they moved their famous Coronation Stone to Scone in the ninth century.

It was captured by Robert the Bruce in 1308, after which he entrusted it to the Campbell Clan and it was added to in the fifteenth century when Alexander II was planning to attack the Viking-held

Dunstaffnage Castle.

Hebrides. In 1746 it became the prison of Flora MacDonald after she had helped Prince Charles Edward – Bonnie Prince Charlie – to escape after Culloden.

When the Campbell family resided in the castle they were watched over by their resident 'fairy'. Although technically the Glaistig was not a conventional fairy she had many fairy traits, including a love of green-coloured dresses, the ability to become invisible and the gift of being able to pass handicraft skills on to those she favoured.

Visiting Information

Situated close to the village of Dunbeg, 5 miles north of Oban, Argyll. Open daily from 1 April to 30 September. Closed Thursdays and Fridays from November to March.

DUNSTANBURGH CASTLE

The site of one of England's oldest ghost stories is Dunstanburgh Castle, now an imposing ruin. Unlike other castles of the Border, Dunstanburgh was not built to protect the marches between England and Scotland. It was built seven centuries ago by Thomas Plantagenet, 2nd Earl of Lancaster, who doubtless realised that a castle on a remote spot on the Northumbria coast could not be bettered as a place of refuge, especially as he devoted himself to opposing Edward II. Yet he refused to flee to Dunstanburgh after the king's victory at the Battle of Borough Bridge with the result that he was captured and beheaded.

After that Dunstanburgh had various castellans including such historic notables as John of Gaunt and Henry Bolingbroke who became the first Lancastrian king. After the Wars of the Roses ended the castle was badly damaged as a result of various sieges and Henry VIII's commissions reported it to be 'very ruinous'. And so it has remained.

The Dunstanburgh legend dates from a time when the castle was already uninhabitable. A knight, known in the story as Sir Guy, was making a journey along the coast when at nightfall he was overtaken by a storm and sought shelter in the ruins.

He had settled his horse under an archway when a glowing figure appeared and a voice that rose above the gale told the knight to follow him if he wished to find a 'beauty bright'. The ghost led Sir Guy through a maze of tunnels beneath the castle and into a huge cavern.

Eerie lights shone on the armour of a hundred warriors who lay entranced by their equally entranced warhorses. At the end of the subterranean hall two skeletal figures guarded a crystal sarcophagus in which lay a beautiful lady like some Sleeping Beauty with a tear glistening on her cheek.

One of the guardians held a sword in its bony fingers and the other a horn. The ghost told the knight that he had to choose the sword or the horn and the fate of himself and the enchanted lady – the 'beauty bright' – would depend on his choice.

It seemed logical to Sir Guy to take the horn to awaken the sleeper. He took it and blew an echoing blast through the hall. The eyes of the

Dunstanburgh Castle.

dormant warriors opened and their horses snorted and stamped their hooves. But as Sir Guy gazed expectantly at the lady in the crystal coffin the scene dissolved into a nightmare and as Sir Guy slipped into unconsciousness a voice – according to a ballad – thundered:

> Shame on the coward who sounded a horn
> When he might have unsheathed a sword!

Sir Guy woke at dawn in the ruins and though he searched for the entrance to the maze in the hope of reaching the beautiful sleeper, he found no clue to the underground hall or the ghost who had led him to it.

Visiting Information
The castle overlooks the sea a mile and a half's walk from Craster, Northumberland. The ruins are open to the public.

DUNTRUNE CASTLE

The story of the Phantom Piper of Duntrune is set in one of Scotland's oldest inhabited castles which was built towards the end of the twelfth century. The story of the piper goes back to 1615, when feuding between the Campbells and MacDonalds was at its height. At this time Call Ciotach, of the MacDonald clan, had captured Duntrune Castle and garrisoned it with his followers, after which he sailed south in his galley to the Isle of Islay.

While he was away the Campbells of Duntrune (who had been masters of the castle for five centuries) counter-attacked and retook the fortress, killing every MacDonald except Coll Ciotach's piper. In those days pipers, because of their musical ability, were regarded as privileged persons like heralds.

What anguished the piper was the knowledge that when his master returned, he would be unaware that the castle was back in the hands of his enemies and he would run straight into an ambush. In a flash of inspiration the piper decided to compose a special pibroch which was to become known as *The Piper's Warning to his Master*.

Some days later the restless gaze of the piper picked out a boat sailing up the Sound of Jura which he recognised as belonging to his master. Taking his pipes, he hurried to the castle's ramparts and began to play. The strange bagpipe music floated over the sound, and in his galley Coll realised that this was no ordinary welcome. There was something wild and urgent about it, something that hinted of danger.

He ordered his rowers to rest while he regarded the castle and the lone figure of the piper silhouetted against the sky. Apart from him, the place seemed deserted. Where were his clansmen who normally would be coming to the shore to greet their leader?

The more Coll puzzled about it and the more he heard the desperate skirl of the pipes the more suspicious he became. He shouted a command to his helmsman, the galley turned and churned back down the sound.

At the castle the MacDonalds, realizing that the loyal piper had robbed them of their prey, seized him and hacked off his hands in savage revenge. He soon died from loss of blood and was buried beneath the castle flagstones. But from then on there have been

Duntrune Castle.

times when his warning pibroch has been heard skirling from the battlements.

Just over a hundred years ago restoration work was undertaken at Duntroon and beneath some timeworn slabs a skeleton was discovered with its fingerbones missing. It was given a proper burial by the Dean of Argyll.

Visiting Information

The castle stands close to Lochgilphead, Argyll. It is owned by the current clan chief of the Clan Malcolm.

DUNVEGAN CASTLE

Dunvegan Castle on the Isle of Skye was the home of a Glaistig, or benign female spirit like that of Dunstaffnage Castle. The castle has been the seat of Clan MacLeod since the beginning of the thirteenth century. Apart from its supernatural benefactor, it is noted for its collection of historical objects which includes relics of Bonnie Prince Charlie and the famous Fairy Flag of the MacLeods.

This banner was credited with the power to bring victory to the clan when waved in battle, to make the marriage of a MacLeod chief fruitful when spread on the nuptial bed, and to attract the herrings in the loch when unfurled.

Legend tells that the flag was given to the clan by a Glaistig who, in the guise of a mortal woman, had married a member of the MacLeod's clan. The gift was made at the nearby Fairy Bridge which still stands. One of the conditions attached to the flag was that it could only be waved three times for military victory. So far the clan has resorted to their talisman twice, once in 1490 at the Battle of Glendale and in 1580 at Trumpan. On both occasions the gift of the Glaistig brought them victory.

Dunvegan is still the clan stronghold and is visited by MacLeods from all over the world who wish to see their ancestral home and their magical flag.

Visiting Information

Situated close to Dunvegan village by the loch of the same name, Isle of Skye. Open to visitors daily from 1 April to 15 October. For groups only by appointment weekdays from 16 October to 31 March.

EDZELL CASTLE

The partly ruined Edzell Castle was once the scene of an extraordinary gypsy's curse that became part of local folklore. The original Norman edifice was the home of the Crawford Lindsays around the fourteenth century, but most of the present castle dates back to the end of the sixteenth century, when Sir David Lindsay carried out an extensive building programme which, if an inscription on of the walls is to be believed, caused him to die in 'extraordinary debt'. His best addition to the castle was a pleasance – a formal walled garden – which, according to official history, 'gives Edzell Castle a distinctive place in the art of the European Renaissance.'

The Edzell Curse goes back to when Lord Crawford had two dumb gypsy boys hanged for poaching on his land. The boys' mother came to the castle and, according to the traditional tale, confronted Lady Crawford. She cried out, 'I curse you! For you, Lady Crawford, you shall not see the sun set. You and the unborn babe you carry will both be buried in the same grave, and for you, Lord Crawford, you shall die a death that would make the boldest man ever born of woman, even to witness, shriek with fear.'

It would seem that this terrible anathema was remarkably effective. Within hours Lady Crawford collapsed and died and soon afterwards her husband was devoured by wolves.

A happier tradition associated with Edzell concerns a lady of the castle who, after a period of illness, fell into a cataleptic trance. Her physician mistook this for death and her sorrowing relatives laid her to rest in the family vault.

Having heard that the lady had been interred wearing her jewellery, the avaricious sexton entered the crypt at night and prised the lid off her coffin. The light of his lantern gleamed on the gold of her ornaments. He plucked them from her body until only her rings were left. Unable to pull them off the rigid fingers he drew his knife and made a clumsy attempt at amputation.

According to an old record the supposed corpse stirred, sat up and murmured 'Alas!' At this, the tomb-robber fainted and collapsed by the coffin. The lady struggled to her feet, revived the sexton and led him into the night air. She was so thankful to be restored that

Edzell Castle.

she asked the sexton to go with her to the castle where her husband would reward him.

Shrewdly guessing the sort of reward he would receive, he ran away and duly emigrated to a foreign land. If it had not been for his greed there might have been a White Lady haunting Edzell today, bewailing the years that she been cheated out of by the faulty diagnosis.

Visiting Information

The castle stands a short distance from Edzell, Angus, on a by-road leading to Witton. Can be hired for ceremonies only.

FEATHERSTONE CASTLE

The setting of one of the most dramatic Border hauntings is Featherstone Castle which stands in parkland close to a stretch of the South Tyne. In past times when local folk were disturbed by the terrified barking of all the dogs in the neighbourhood they used to say 'The riders of Featherstone are abroad tonight.' They were referring to a ghostly cavalcade known as the Phantom Hunt.

The oldest part of the castle dates back to at least 1212, when Helios de Featherstonehaugh owned the estate which was to remain the seat of his descendants for many generations. Through the centuries the original square pele tower was added to so that today it is a romantic mixture of styles which included a crenellated curtain wall and a couple of watch towers. Final additions, including a low surrounding wall, were completed early in the nineteenth century when the Wallace family took over the estate.

The castle's legend goes back to when Abigail, the beautiful only child of the last Baron Featherstonehaugh, fell in love with young Ridley of nearby Hard Riding. It was an unfortunate choice as her old father was determined that she should marry a distant relative to cement a Border alliance.

After the reluctant girl had submitted to the nuptial ceremony the wedding guests decided to celebrate with a hunt; in the priorities of the rough Border lords the chase was second only to feuding. Only the old baron, who perhaps had celebrated the outcome of his plan with over much wassail, and his wife remained in the Featherstone hall.

Away to the north streamed the hunters until they reached a gloomy wood called Pynkinscleugh where they expected to find deer. Instead they looked up to the high ground of the cleugh and saw the grim figure of Ridley at the head of his armed retainers.

'Give up the Lady Abigail or I shall carry her away over your bodies,' he shouted.

'No Ridley shall take my bride,' retorted the bridegroom.

Unsheathing his sword the rejected suitor rode down on the wedding guests. While the vassals from Hard Riding and the vassals from Featherstone took each others' lives on behalf of their masters, Ridley engaged in single combat with the bridegroom.

Featherstone Castle.

Distraught at the sight of her lover and her new husband slashing at each other, the bride rushed between then – and was fatally struck with a sword. The suitor and the husband continued to fight over her body until both fell mortally wounded. Ridley collapsed over a bowl-shaped rock into which his blood flowed. In the silence that followed ill-omened ravens gathered round and dipped their beaks into the warm blood, giving it the name of the Ravens' Rock. It can still be seen in the heart of the lonely wood.

Back at Featherstone Castle, the baron woke at midnight while his wife dozed in her chair beside him. Suddenly he hauled himself to his feet to greet his guests as they walked silently into the hall. Then to his horror he saw that each was disfigured with dreadful wounds, each face had the pallor of death, and all moved through the furniture as though it did not exist. Automatically the baron crossed himself and the ghastly company faded away.

According to the legend, the baron went insane with the realisation that his daughter and the bridal party had returned as ghosts. The Phantom Hunt is believed to re-enact its return to Featherstone Castle at midnight on each anniversary of the ambush and in doing so strikes terror into the neighbourhood dogs.

The castle is said to have two other ghosts. One is that of Sir Reginald FitzUrse who, as a prisoner in the old tower, was starved to death and whose groans are said to have occasionally been heard.

The other is the spectre of a mysterious Green Lady who makes an appearance from time to time but whose story remains a mystery.

Visiting Information

Overlooking the South Tyne, the castle can be reached by road a short distance from Haltwhistle, Northumberland. On private land but good external viewing.

FYVIE CASTLE

Fyvie Castle is famed as 'the crowning glory of Scottish baronial architecture'. It is also notable for its tradition of ghostly phenomena which was once summed up in an article printed in *The Times* which read:

> Like the Castle of Glamis it has a secret chamber; like the Palace of Holyrood, it has a 'murder room', with ineffaceable blood-stains on the floor. It has its spirit that haunts the great vaulted staircase, bringing warnings of death and disaster like the Irish banshee; and signs and portents are to be sought and found in the very stones of the ancient battlements.

The castle was built in the fifteenth century, when the lands of Fyvie were awarded to Henry de Preston for his valour in capturing an English knight, Sir Ralph Percy at the Battle of Otterburn in 1388. The tower he built is still known as the Preston Tower.

In the sixteenth century the castle was sold to Alexander Seton, who became Lord Fyvie and Lord High Chancellor of Scotland. He also served as a tutor to Charles I, who had been born at Dunfermline, and his family was to remain faithful to the Stewart cause. His son Charles paid for his loyalty by having his land seized by Parliament in 1648 but they were returned with the Restoration.

The next private owner of Fyvie was the Earl of Aberdeen, chief of the Gordon Clan, who purchased it in 1726, and it was the Gordons who feared a phantom trumpeter.

Among the statues which decorate the roofs of Fyvie is one of a man blowing a trumpet said to be one Andrew Lammie who was employed at the castle as a trumpeter. He fell in love with a girl named Agnes, the daughter of a local miller. Her parents disapproved of the young man and persuaded the Gordon owner of the castle to banish him to Edinburgh. The unhappy parting of the lovers inspired the statue.

There is nothing sinister about that story but there is in another version. In the second version, one of the lords of Fyvie was greatly attracted by the daughter of his steward, but found that the girl preferred the young trumpeter and had agreed to marry him. In order to get his humble rival out of the way he arranged for him to be taken by a press gang to sea and an unknown fate. Soon afterwards the girl died of a broken heart. After that the spirit of Andrew Lammie returned to the castle to blow an unearthly blast on his trumpet whenever the chief of the Gordons was about to die.

Another ghost said to presage ill luck for the owners of the castle is the Green Lady of Fyvie. Her story goes back to 1596, when Alexander Seton bought the castle. Four years earlier he had married a lady named Lilias Drummond and he was constantly hoping for a son to whom he would hand on the family name and the castle. But his eagerness turned to desperation as each of his wife's pregnancies ended with the birth of a daughter.

Then, in May 1601, Lilias died and in October Lord Fyvie married Grizel Leslie, the daughter of his late wife. On their wedding night they were awakened by a strange sighing outside the window panes. That morning they might have dismissed it as gust of winds except that they saw two words incised on the stone window ledge – *LILIAS DRUMMOND.*

The window was so high up in the castle wall it seemed impossible that someone could have climbed up to the ledge and if he had the noise of his hammer and chisel would have surely drawn attention to his activities.

At the time people were ready to accept a supernatural explanation and down the years strange stories have been told. They centred on a small panelled out-of-the-way apartment which for generations was known as the Murder Room. One legend states this room was the prison for a lady whose reason for incarceration ranged from the revenge of a jealous husband to her responsibility for a crime so hideous its nature was kept secret.

The ghost of the Green Lady of Fyvie is seen in a corridor and on the staircase that led to the Murder Room. She has been described as holding a candle, while pearls decorate her hair and pale light shimmers from her green brocade dress. She always disappears in the remote room. Her appearance was said to herald ill fortune for the owners of the castle.

Apart from supernatural visitations, the castle has had the curse of the Weeping Stones of Fyvie hanging over it. The malediction was pronounced by Thomas of Ercildoun.

Mentioned on other pages, Thomas the Rhymer, as he was known, was famous for his predictions. These were usually doom-laden, and doubtless many a noble lord dreaded the arrival of the old man at his gate with some doggerel lines reeking of misfortune.

On one occasion he arrived in a howling gale at Fyvie where, according to one version of the story, he was furious at not being allowed to sing his minstrel songs in the castle hall. Perhaps the lord of Fyvie had no wish to listen to the wizard's gloomy prophecies.

Whatever the reason Thomas uttered an imprecation which included the lines:

> Hapless shall your mesdames be
> When ye shall hae within your methes,
> Frae harryit kirks lands, stanes
> Three ...

The word 'methes' in those far off days meant boundary stones and 'harrykit kirks lands' suggest they marked the boundary between Church land and the Fyvie estate.

The usual interpretation of the strange pronouncement was if the stones were moved no male heir would be born within the castle walls, a state of affairs said to have held good after Henry de Preston sacrilegiously moved the stones to use in renovating the castle.

They earned the 'Weeping Stones' title because they became mysteriously bedewed when plundered from the boundary with the Church, the local people declaring they were weeping at the impiety of the act. Afterwards one of the stones was said to weep whenever ill fortune threatened the master of the castle.

Visiting Information

Situated a short distance north of the village of Fyvie, Grampian. Garden open all year, castle open 1 April to 31 October.

GLAMIS CASTLE

There is no doubt about the reality of the noises at Glamis castle. On one occasion, some years ago, the head of the family, with several companions, was determined to investigate the cause. One night, when the disturbance was greater and more violent than usual, and it should be premised strange, weird and unearthly sounds had often been heard, and by many persons, some quite unacquainted with the ill repute of the Castle, his lordship went to the Haunted Room, opened the door with a key and dropped back in a dead swoon into the arms of his companions; nor could he ever be induced to open his lips on the subject afterwards.

What a classic introduction for a ghost story, especially as Glamis Castle is one of the world's best-known haunted sites. It is also Scotland's oldest inhabited castle.

The description of the opening of the sealed room appeared in the Revd F.G. Lee's *Glimpses of the Supernatural*, published in 1875, but it is merely the iceberg's tip of the castle's macabre legends. For the annual tourist pilgrimage it has the added attraction of being the family home of the late Queen Elizabeth, the Queen Mother, whose ancestors held it for six centuries.

Legend tells that Macbeth, the Thane of Glamis, stabbed Duncan in a gloomy chamber still known as Duncan's Hall. Some scholars have suggested that Shakespeare may have visited the spot when travelling to Aberdeen with a group of actors.

Another claimant for Macbeth is the also haunted Cawdor Castle, but Duncan died in 1040, three centuries before Cawdor was built. It is known that another king, Malcolm II, was assassinated at Glamis, seven years before Duncan.

Apart from the Macbeth episode, little is known of the castle's history until 1372, when Sir John Lyon, the Baron of Fortevist and the Great Chamberlain of Scotland, married Joanna the daughter of Robert II, and gained Glamis for a tribute of 'one red falcon to be delivered yearly on the Feast of Pentecost'.

Known as the 'White Lyon' because of his pale features, Sir John brought with him an heirloom in the form of a cup which was regarded a symbol of the family's luck. The word 'doom' should

Glamis Castle.

be substituted for 'luck' as, according to legend, taking it from its original home was responsible for the ill fortune which followed its arrival at Glamis.

No doubt the cup was blamed in 1383 when Sir John Lyon was killed in a duel. And again in 1537 when Janet Douglas, widow of the 6th Lord of Glamis, was accused of attempting to kill James V of Scotland by witchcraft in company with her son and her second husband Archibald Campbell of Skipnish. He fell to his death while trying to escape from Edinburgh Castle.

His end was merciful compared to that of his wife who was burned at the stake on Castle Hill 'with great commiseration of the people, being in the prime of years, of a singular beauty, and suffering all, though being a woman, with manlike courage.'

The spectre of the unfortunate lady has since been seen surrounded by a lurid halo floating above the castle clock tower.

The new young lord of Glamis was more fortunate than his parents. Although sentenced to death with his mother for plotting against the king, the court suspended the sentence until he should reach his twenty-first birthday. By this time William Lyon, a malicious relative who had laid the charges against the family, made a death-bed confession that he had acted out of spite. The prisoner was released and his estates restored to him.

Some believed that the strange knocking which from time to time reverberated through part of the castle is the ghostly echo of the hammering which accompanied the building of Lady Janet's scaffold.

Another, and more horrific, story about the knocking is that it goes back to the time when there was a bloody feud between the Lindsays and the Ogilvies. Following a battle between the two clans, a band of defeated Ogilvie retainers arrived at Glamis and begged for protection. The lord of the castle did not want to fall foul of the desperate fugitives, nor did he want to antagonise the Lindsays by helping their enemies. So he invited the men in and conducted them to a remote room where he told them they would be safe. Then he locked them in. According to one legend, they were not found until Victorian times when Lord Strathmore unlocked the door and fainted. It is suggested that what he saw was a mound of skeletons, some of which still had their bony arms between their teeth as starvation had driven them to eat their own flesh.

The tradition of the castle's secret room was described by Sir Walter Scott who, in writing about Glamis, said, 'It contains also a curious monument of the peril of feudal times, being a secret chamber; the entrance of which, by law or custom of the family, must only be known to three persons at once, viz. the Earl of Strathmore, his heir apparent, and any third person whom they may take into their confidence.

Of the various theories advanced as to the secret of the hidden room, the most popular is that a terribly deformed child – the result of a curse laid on the family – was hidden away in it. A typical example of this story appeared in the *Daily Telegraph* of 28 October 1966:

> The walls in the old castle are immensely thick – up to 15 feet in places. Somewhere in them lies the secret of Glamis – a mysterious chamber where a previous Earl is supposed to have kept hidden a hideous monster, a son born half man, half beast.

For 150 years the monster lived in the castle, only emerging to crawl about at night.

One historical fact adds to the legend. A portrait in the drawing room shows the 1st Earl with his sons: two boys and a peculiar little dwarf.

Apart from the secret room, Glamis Castle abounds with ghosts. A White Lady has been seen gliding along the avenue to the castle, as has a tall spectral figure nicknamed 'Jack the Runner', while a young black boy, a page who was cruelly treated, has materialised close to the door of the sitting room used by the Queen Mother.

Visiting Information

Situated close to Glamis village, south-west of Forfar, Perthshire. Open April to December.

GOODRICH CASTLE

Described as one of Britain's most picturesque medieval ruins, Goodrich Castle stands on a mound in the centre of a huge moat. It was built in the thirteenth century on the site of an earlier fortification known as Godric's Castle which commanded a ford in the adjacent river.

Nothing remains of Godric's Castle but the moat which was hewn out of solid rock and which probably followed the lines of its wall. The first recorded owner of the castle was the Earl of Pembroke, but in the early part of the fourteenth century the castle passed by marriage to the Talbot family who, as the Earls of Shrewsbury, held it until it was finally deserted.

When the Civil War broke out Parliamentary troops garrisoned the castle briefly before it passed back into the hands of the Royalists who, under Sir Henry Lingen, were soon defending it against the Roundheads again. The leader of the Parliamentary forces, Colonel Birch, made a surprise attack but was beaten back having only managed to burn some stables. He raised the siege but returned in 1646 as the castle was still defended by men loyal to King Charles. They clung to their lost cause until their water supply was cut off. After their surrender the castle was slighted by cannon fire.

The haunting of the castle goes back to Colonel Birch's siege. His niece, Alice, was in love with a young Royalist sympathiser named Clifford, and together they found refuge in the castle. When her uncle's first attack failed Alice must have believed they were safe.

Then came the news of the king's surrender to the Scots at Newark in May 1646. This was followed by the return of Colonel Birch with more artillery, including huge mortar capable of throwing cannon balls weighing 200lb into the beleaguered castle.

As the days passed and bombardments shook the castle, Clifford and Alice realised it would be only a matter of time before the combined effects of thirst and cannon fire would force the defenders to surrender. Equally depressing for the Royalists was the news that the Scots were planning to sell King Charles to the Parliamentarians for £400,000. One night, when storm clouds obscured the moon, Clifford saddled his horse and, with Alice beside him, managed to lead it out of the castle unnoticed. On the other side of the moat he

Goodrich Castle.

mounted and, with Alice riding pillion, they spurred through the lines of sleeping Roundheads to plunge down the steep slope that led to the River Wye. Here they hoped to cross at the ford and make their escape.

They had not bargained on the heavy rain which had caused the river to flood. A moment after Clifford had urged his reluctant mount into the water they were swept away to their deaths.

Since then, when storms lash the castle's shattered towers, the tragic cries of Alice and Clifford ring above the howl of the wind.

On the anniversary of the tragedy a horseman, with a lady mounted behind him, have been seen to enter the river at the ford and then disappear beneath the dark current.

For following centuries this spot was shunned by courting couples who feared that the melancholy fate of Clifford and Alice would overshadow their own happiness.

Visiting Information

The castle is situated half a mile north from Goodrich on the A40, Herefordshire. See the website for family events throughout the summer.

GREYSTOKE CASTLE

Behind its Elizabethan façade looms the original square pele tower of Greystoke Castle, which had been built by William Lord Greystoke in 1353. It is to this old tower that the Greystoke ghost has returned from time to time, a ghost whose departure from life was more mysterious than its subsequent hauntings.

When Charles Howard, Duke of Norfolk, was master of Greystoke he invited a friend to stay at the castle to enjoy a hunt with him. After a day in the field and a convivial supper, the guest retired to his room in the old pele tower.

He did not come to breakfast but the duke took little notice of this. The exertion of the hunt, or perhaps the celebration after it, had probably caused the guest to sleep longer than usual. But when he did not appear by midday, his host sent a servant to rouse him.

The man reported that the guest was not in the room. Furthermore, he could not have left the castle because his clothes were still hanging over the back of a chair. The duke immediately went to the tower and found everything as he had been told. The bed had been slept in, and the clothes were hanging as the servant had described, but of his

Greystoke Castle.

friend there was no sign. The castle staff were ordered to search the whole building and the grounds around it, but no clue was found as to the riddle of the vanishing guest who was never heard of again.

The room remained untenanted from then on, apart from the phantom of the missing gentleman which unfortunately has thrown no light on the mystery of his fate.

Another ghost is connected with the same room, manifesting itself by knocking on the wall as though it was desperately trying to break through. It is said to be the echo of an errant monk who was walled up in an underground passage which led from the tower to a chapel in the castle grounds.

Visiting Information

Situated at Greystoke, west of Penrith, Cumbria. On private land.

HASTINGS CASTLE

When William, Duke of Normandy, landed at Pevensey Bay in October 1066, he brought with him prefabricated wooden forts. The Bayeux Tapestry shows that one was taken to Hastings and erected on a hastily raised motte (a prominent part of the castle today), and thus the first Norman castle was built in Britain. Three years later the quaintly termed Rape of Hastings was granted to Robert, Count of Eu, who replaced the wooden fort with a stone castle, and a collegiate church was built within its walls.

The mysterious sound heard in the ruins of Hastings Castle goes back to its ecclesiastical days. It is the swell of organ music which issues from the ruins of the castle church.

More sinister are the sounds that come from the dungeons which were hewn out of part of the castle known as The Mount. These ghostly echoes are the clank of chains and moans of starving prisoners. The castle also has a visual ghost said to be of Thomas a Becket who was once a Dean of the Church college there. He appears

Hastings Castle.

within the precincts only on autumnal evenings. Perhaps he is listening for the phantom organ music.

There is an old tradition that when the sun is bright but mist covers the sea, a replica of the castle is occasionally seen as though floating on the horizon. This might be explained as a mirage except that the sea castle is not ruined – it appears as it must have been in its heyday with banners billowing above its towers.

Visiting Information

The ruins of Hastings Castle can be seen at the town of the same name in Sussex. Open to the public.

HAUGHTON CASTLE

Death by neglect has left a ghostly aftermath at Haughton Hall whose towers look across the North Tyne in Northumberland. The haunting goes back to the days when Sir John Widdrington was lord of the castle.

At that time the Border was a lawless place, made worse by the fact that Lord Dacre of Gilsland had been appointed Lord Warden of the Marches. Instead of pacifying the area, he was known to be in league with the freebooting families who preyed on their neighbours.

The oppressed local gentry asked Sir John to travel to York to inform Cardinal Wolsey of the unhappy situation.

Just before Sir John began his journey his retainers captured a reiver named Archie Armstrong. He was summarily thrown into a dungeon and Sir John, his head full of the importance of his mission, rode off. It was only when he reached York that he found the key of the dungeon in his pocket and realised with a thrill of horror the

Haughton Castle.

plight of the prisoner for it was the only key in existence that could unlock the massive dungeon door. He immediately began the return journey, galloping so fast that when he reached Durham one horse had died beneath him. When he finally arrived at the castle his first words were to ask about the prisoner. The retainers answered that for the first two days there had been a lot of shouting from behind the oaken door but latterly there had been silence.

Sir John ran to the door, turned the key in the lock and found Archie Armstrong sprawled on the floor dead from thirst.

As a protest of his untimely end the phantom of the outlaw returned to Haughton Castle, and his despairing cries rang again and again from the dungeon to torment the inhabitants and drive away the servants. A minister was called to exorcise the spirit, and the ceremony appeared to be successful. The Bible that had been used in the ritual was kept within the castle as a protection against the spirit's return.

Years later it was found that the leather binding of the book was crumbling and it was despatched to London for rebinding. Almost immediately after it had gone the dying cries of Archie Armstrong were heard again in the castle. A messenger was sent urgently to London to bring back the book, after which peace was restored.

Visiting Information

Situated in the bank of the North Tyne 2 miles from Humshaugh, Northumberland. On private land.

HERMITAGE CASTLE

S ir Walter Scott, who regarded Hermitage as his favourite castle, wrote thus of its reputation in local folklore: 'The Castle of Hermitage unable to support the load of iniquity which had long been accumulating within its walls, is supposed to have partly sunk beneath the ground; and its ruins are still regarded by the peasants with peculiar aversion and horror.'

Hermitage was built in the thirteenth century to guard the western approach to Scotland. In the fourteenth century a Scottish historian, John of Fordon, wrote that in 1242 England nearly came to war because the Scots had erected in Liddesdale 'a certain castle which is called Hermitage.'

Another early account states in the year 1300 Edward I ordered it to be repaired at the cost of £20, and in the century which followed possession of the castle frequently changed hands between the Scots and English. In 1338 it was captured by Sir William Douglas, the famous knight of Liddesdale, after which followed a good deal of confusion and mayhem.

Four years after taking the castle Sir William starved his prisoner, the previous owner of Hermitage, to death. When he changed sides and threw in his lot with the English, King David II of Scotland gave the castle to another William, later the 1st Earl of Douglas. He guaranteed his right to the property by murdering Sir William Douglas in Ettrick Forest. Sir William's widow then married a member of the Dacre family who, with the might of Edward III behind him, took the castle back into English hands.

By 1371 the Douglases were once more masters of Hermitage, holding it until 1492 when James IV, of Scotland, suspected the current owner of treachery. The king forced him to exchange Hermitage for a castle on the Clyde where he could be kept under royal scrutiny.

There must have been something about the castle which inspired dark ambition as the new lord of Hermitage began to conspire with the English. Yet despite the taint of suspicion which always surrounded them, the Bothwells managed to retain the castle for 102 years. The most famous member of the family was the 4th earl who became Mary Queen of Scots' lover. The 5th earl was attainted and

Hermitage Castle.

forced to surrender the castle to Elizabeth I, after which its role in Border history lessened and by the eighteenth century it had become a ruin.

With such a tradition of treachery and bloodshed it is only to be expected that the gaunt shell gained the reputation of being haunted. The ghost is that of one of the castle's first owners, Lord William de Soulis, who in the thirteenth century was the hereditary King's Butler of Scotland.

According to legend, his phantom returns once every seven years to Hermitage where, in an underground chamber, he keeps a tryst with an evil spirit. Lord de Soulis, whose wickedness eclipsed that of any of the lords who followed him, had an arch enemy in the huge Cout of Keilder – the name 'Cout' being a local word meaning 'colt' so the nickname suggests someone fast and strong.

The Cout had a suit of armour whose magical properties ensured that its owner was invincible in combat. Wearing it, he rode up to Hermitage one day and roared a challenge to its high walls. He did not have to wait long before the figure of Lord de Soulis appeared to take up the gauntlet.

Broadsword clashed against broadsword but although Lord de Soulis was a more skilful fighter his blows seemed to have no effect on his enemy. He felt his sword vibrate strangely each time it struck the Cout's armour and he realised he was facing powers he did not understand.

Lord de Soulis had no objection to ignoring the rules of chivalry and he called upon his relatives to come to his aid. When the Cout saw a determined band of warriors emerge from the castle he fled towards Hermitage Water. Here his pursuers flung him down the bank and, aware that conventional weapons could not injure him, held his head under the water until the bubbles ceased to issue from his magic helmet.

Nearby the castle is a mound marked with 'tippet stones' which is said to be the grave of the drowned baron.

Having seen the effectiveness of magic, Lord de Soulis determined to become a master of the art. For his sorcery he used the blood of kidnapped children to summon up an evil spirit known in local tradition as Robin Redcap, the cap getting its colour from the human blood in which it was steeped. This vampirish familiar guaranteed that Lord de Soulis could not be killed by steel or hemp, therefore he was safe from hanging or injury by iron weapons.

Believing himself to be invincible, the terrible lord of Hermitage committed outrage after outrage without fear of retribution. Finally the local people could take no more – rumours of the fate of the unusually large number of missing children began to circulate, so they sought the advice of a famous wizard, Thomas Ercildoune, who told them how they could dispose of the tyrant without his familiar being able to protect him.

The peasants of Liddesdale seized the wicked lord and knowing that he was proof against their ropes and billhooks they followed the advice of the wizard described in an old ballad:

> On a circle of stones they place the pot,
> On a circle of stones but barely nine;
> They heated it red and fiery hot,
> And the burnished brass did glimmer
> And shine.

> They rolled him up in a sheet of lead
> A sheet of lead for a funeral pall;
> They plunged him into the cauldron red,
> And melted him, body, lead, bones,
> And all.

But though the wicked lord may have been melted down, his spirit still had to rendezvous with Robin Redcap every seven years in an underground chamber of the castle where he once performed his bloody rites. Legend tells that he gave the castle key to the spirit and with it the secret of his ill-gotten treasure.

Visiting Information

Situated close to the village of Hermitage, 20 miles south of Hawick, Roxburghshire. Open April to September.

HERSTMONCEAUX CASTLE

A castle famous for its phantom drummer is Herstmonceaux, south of the Sussex village of that name. Thanks to restoration work in 1933, it appears remarkably new which is fitting as it has housed the Royal Observatory since 1948 when the atmosphere above Greenwich became too polluted for star-gazing. The castle was built in the fifteenth century by Sir Roger de Fiennes, a hero of Agincourt and later Henry VI's treasurer, who was created Lord Dacre.

The ghost is believed to have been one of Sir Roger's followers whose drumming rolled over the Agincourt battlefield before he was struck down. Such was his loyalty to his master his shade returned to Herstmonceaux to re-enact over the centuries his obligation to the hubbub of the battle – to the fear of the locals who regarded the occasional drumbeats as an ill-omen.

Another story tells how a certain elderly Lord Dacre developed a morbid enthusiasm for religion and emulated early Christian anchorites who tried to escape temptation by hiding themselves away from the world. To this end he retired to a small cell in the castle where he lived on bread and water in true hermitical tradition. In order to protect his young and vivacious wife from admirers eager to console a lonely lady he beat a drum at night in the hope that superstitious fear of the drummer would deter them.

The situation so infuriated Lady Dacre that she locked the door of the recluse's cell and left him to starve to death. But the phantom drummer continued to beat his drum.

Herstmonceaux has other ghosts, including an heiress who also starved to death. To prevent her inheriting her rightful property, her governess was bribed to lure her to a remote chamber and imprison her. The girl died of hunger on the eve of her twenty-first birthday and since then her emaciated shade has appeared by the edge of the moat.

The appearance of four spectral huntsmen galloping in the castle's vicinity goes back to 1542 when wild Lord Dacre and three boon companions went for a midnight hunt on a neighbouring estate. Close by Cuckmere River they were challenged by a gamekeeper who ordered them off. The trespassers drew their swords and the

Herstmonceaux Castle.

gamekeeper was mortally wounded, but before he died he named his assailants with the result they were charged with murder and executed.

Visiting Information

The castle is situated a short distance south of Herstmonceaux, Sussex. Open April to October.

HEVER CASTLE

Hever Castle has many attractions for the visitor. These include a maze and a smuggler's cave in its spacious grounds, but above all it has the ghost of Anne Boleyn.

Nearly five centuries have passed since her execution in the Tower of London, yet her fascination as a woman and a historical character remains. The love Henry VIII felt for her led to the English Reformation, she became the mother of Elizabeth I, and her death at the age of thirty-two placed her among the tragic but fascinating quartet of British queens who have knelt at the headsman's block.

Work began on Hever Castle towards the end of the thirteenth century and two centuries later a Tudor house was completed within its walls by Sir Thomas Boleyn. His daughter Anne, just returned from the French court, met King Henry in the castle garden. His passion for her began in 1522, though he continued to treat his wife Queen Catherine of Aragon with suitable respect.

From the example of Elizabeth Woodville's association with Edward IV, Anne knew that virtue could sometimes be more profitable than vice and she determined not to emulate her sister who had been the king's mistress. If Henry wanted her he would have to marry her!

Henry rejoiced in wooing an elusive lady. It was different from anything he had experienced before. He wrote lengthy letters to her and composed a poem in which he compared her to a holly, part of which ran:

> Now unto my lady
> Promise to her I make
> For all other only
> To her I me betake.

His sentiments showed more vividly when he wrote:

> Mine own sweetheart, this shall be to advertise you of the great elengeness [loneliness] that I find here since your departing. I think your kindness and my fervencies of love causeth it ... Wishing myself (especially of an evening) in my sweetheart's arms, whose pretty dukkys I facet shortly to kiss.

Hever Castle.

While Henry strove to divorce his queen, Anne was created Marchioness of Pembroke, travelled with the royal retinue and had her own apartments. When she knew she had sufficient hold on the king she allowed him her favours, and was pregnant when Henry secretly married her in January 1533. With the Reformation under way, the Convocation obediently acknowledged the invalidity of Henry's marriage to his first wife and Archbishop Cranmer confirmed the king's marriage to Anne. In June he placed the crown on her head.

Yet within three months Henry's love began to cool and the birth in September of a daughter named Elizabeth did not revive it. The next year Anne's hopes of producing an heir were dashed when she had a miscarriage, and the king solaced himself by falling in love with one of Anne's maids of honour, Jane Seymour. After this Anne's progress to the Tower was inevitable.

Following her execution Anne's spectre has been seen to glide over a bridge which spans the River Eden at Hever Castle. On each occasion the appearance of the royal spectre has been reported on Christmas Eve.

Visiting Information

Situated close to the village of Hever, south-east of Edenbridge, Kent. Open April to October. For the winter season see website.

HUNTINGTOWER CASTLE

O f female ghosts mentioned in this book, the most benign is the one who haunts Huntingtower Castle. She is claimed to have cured the sick and given friendly warnings to the castle's inhabitants when they were about to be faced with ill fortune. As with the Claypotts ghost, it is hard to say who she was in life but the castle has enough rough history to provide any amount of legends to accommodate her.

Huntingtower was known as Ruthven Castle until the beginning of the sixteenth century. As Ruthven it was the scene of a romantic episode which is still commemorated in 'The Maiden's Leap', a wide gap between two towers. It came about when one of the Ruthven daughters made a terrifying leap from one tower to the other so that she would not be found in her lover's bedroom.

There was a happy ending to the exploit as, according to an old account, 'the fair woman chose not to repeat the leap and the next night eloped and was married.' Other events associated with the castle were less pleasant. The third Lord Ruthven was one of the assassins who killed David Rizzio, the favourite of Mary Queen of Scots, in 1566. His son William witnessed Mary abdicate her throne at Loch Leven Castle and later as Treasurer of Scotland he became Earl of Gowrie.

In 1582 the castle was the scene of the Earl of Gowrie's kidnapping of young James VI of Scotland. As a captive the king was forced by a party of nobles to sanction the imprisonment of his favourite, the Earl of Arran. He was restored when a counterplot freed the king the following year.

In 1585 King James had his revenge when the Earl of Gowrie was beheaded at Stirling. The castle was later restored to the earl's son who died at an early age, and who was followed by John, the last Earl of Gowrie, who was believed to be a necromancer.

He was killed in Perth with his brother Alexander in 1600 for attempting to assassinate the king. Afterwards their bodies were hanged, drawn and quartered in Edinburgh. Perhaps it was the fact the Earl John was credited with being adept in witchcraft that King James developed a morbid interest in the subject and wrote a book about it entitled *Daemonologie*.

After this the castle's name Ruthven was changed to Huntingtower and for a while remained the property of the Crown. But, fascinating as this may be to student of history, it still leaves the origins of the castle's friendly ghost as mysterious as ever.

Visiting Information

Situated a short distance north-west of Perth the castle stands close to the village of Huntingtower, Perthshire. Open daily April to October. Closed Thursdays and Fridays, November to March.

HYLTON CASTLE

All that remains of this castle, built by William de Hylton in the fifteenth century, is a gatehouse surmounted by four turrets with machicolations and faced with a double row of perpendicular-style windows which resulted from alterations made a century ago.

Once the castle was the home of a brownie, not a junior girl guide but a mischievous domestic sprite similar to the house elf in the Harry Potter film. Because of his lack of warm garments he was known as the Cauld Lad of Hylton. According to the traditional account the castle servants, tired of his nightly pranks in the kitchen, decided to get rid of him.

They did this by leaving him a little green cloak and hood as it was believed in those days that if such an elf accepted a gift, and kept it until dawn, he had to decamp. At midnight the brownie appeared, dressed himself in the warm cloak and happily pranced about the kitchen oblivious of the passage of time. His euphoria ended when a cock crowed, upon which he cried:

> Here's a cloak and here's a hood,
> The Cauld Lad o'Hylton will do no more good.

He then disappeared and his name seems to have been transferred to a youth who was killed in the castle and whose ghost sought retribution there.

The real name of the lad was Robert Skelton, and he was employed as a groom. One day in July 1609 fiery Sir Robert Hylton ordered him to the stables to saddle up his horse – and be quick about it. Minutes passed, and the impatient knight went to the stables where he saw Skelton dawdling at his work. In a rage Hylton gave him a fatal blow with a hay-fork, and when he realised what he had done he hid the body under straw until it was safe to remove it and throw it into a pond.

A coroner's inquest was held on Skelton and Sir Robert was accused of murdering him. He was tried and found guilty but in the following September he received a pardon.

But from then on the curse of the Cauld Lad plagued the Hyltons. The crash of poltergeist mayhem resounded through the castle,

Hylton Castle.

trees on the estate would suddenly shake violently in a phantom wind when those about them were still, and such an atmosphere of terror pervaded the room in which the groom had slept none dared to enter it.

The haunting of the Hyltons continued until 1703 when the pond by the castle was drained and the skeleton of a youth was discovered. Following the discovery the last of the Hyltons died and the curse of the Cauld Lad was lifted from the castle.

Of particular interest to visitors from the USA is the so-called Washington Shield carved above the gate depicting stars and stripes.

Visiting Information

Situated close to Castletown on the western side of Sunderland, County Durham. Open daily.

INVERARAY CASTLE

Ghosts, a phantom army and portents of approaching death are part of the legendary history of Inveraray Castle. In the mid-eighteenth century the castle was redesigned as an example of the neo-Gothic revival, giving a façade to the older part of the building which goes back a further two and a half centuries. It is the hereditary seat of the Dukes of Argyll, chiefs of Clan Campbell.

Prior to the death of one of these chiefs, ravens were wont to wheel about the castle in unusual numbers, but a more dramatic portent was described by Mr H.W. Hill, one-time secretary of the English Church Union, in *Lord Halifax's Ghost Book*.

He recalled that in 1913 he dined with Niall Campbell just after the death of his father Lord Archibald Campbell. During the meal the subject of omens came up, Mr Hill mentioning that the ominous gathering of ravens that had been described in the Scottish Press.

Niall Campbell said he believed in the authenticity of the tradition and added that a much more mysterious sign was the galley that sailed over Loch Fyne just prior to his father's death. The vessel, shaped like the ship which is part of the Campbell arms, had three silent figures standing on board as it sailed up the loch and then continued its voyage silent overland to vanish at a spot associated with St Columba, which had been given to the Church by the Campbells.

It was believed that the phantom galley made this journey when the head of the clan was about to die, and on the occasion of Lord Archibald's death it had been seen by many witnesses – not all had the Celtic blood which is often a requirement for the 'second sight' in recognising such portents. An Englishman seeing the galley sail over the shore of the loch shouted, 'Look at that funny airship!'

Apart from the ravens and the galley, Inveraray Castle is haunted by a phantom harper who was executed by order of the Marquis of Montrose when he drove Lord Argyll from his castle in 1644.

The ghost, which has been described as 'a harmless little old thing', appears in Campbell tartan. Apart from his plaintive harping, he makes a noise in the Green Library as though books are being flung about, though when anyone goes to investigate the disturbance they find every volume in place.

Inveraray Castle.

Inveraray was also the scene of an extraordinary phenomenon on 10 July 1758, when the famous physician Sir William Hart was walking in the castle grounds accompanied by a friend and servant. One of the men looked up at the sky and gave an exclamation of amazement. The other two followed his gaze and saw a battle taking place above them. Many of the visionary soldiers wore the uniform of the Highlanders and were desperately attacking a fort defended by a French garrison.

Soon afterwards two ladies, the Miss Campbells of Ederin, arrived at Inveraray breathless with what they had to tell. They had been walking on a nearby road when they saw the vision of a battle in the sky. They described exactly the same spectacle as the three men had seen.

There was great speculation as to what it could mean. At that time England was at war with the French in America, and it was known that Highlanders were stationed at Albany. The nature of the battle was not known until weeks later when an official bulletin stated that Highlanders had been in action against a French fort at Ticonderoga on Lake George and had lost over 300 men killed and as many wounded. The date of the battle was 10 July – the same date that the five people had seen its mysterious 'mirage' in the sky above the castle.

Visiting Information

Situated close to Inveraray on the west side of Loch Fyne, Argyll. Open daily 1 April to 31 October.

JEDBURGH CASTLE

Today Jedburgh Castle is mainly of interest as the present building was a county jail constructed in 1832 to the plan of prison reformer John Howard. The original castle was built in the twelfth century and later became a residence for the kings of Scotland – and it was here that a mysterious apparition materialised at a royal wedding feast.

In October 1285 Alexander II was married to Jolande, the daughter of the Count of Dreux. It was an important marriage for the king and for Scotland. Alexander had been married before but he was still without an heir when his wife died. He knew that unless he married again and had a son Scotland would be doomed to bitter struggles for the succession at his death. Therefore there was great hope in his heart when he stood beside his beautiful bride in the midst of extravagant festivities at Jedburgh. Wine flowed, and the music of minstrels filled the hall.

Suddenly there was a break in the chatteras and all eyes turned to see a tall cowled figure which had suddenly appeared in the midst of the wedding feast guests without announcement. The music stopped. Talking died away as the atmosphere became suddenly cold.

The uninvited stranger stood still and silent and the guests were filled with dread. Then the monk-like figure, which had caused such instant consternation, vanished as suddenly as it had appeared. It was feared that this ghostly visitation was an evil portent – and so it was regarded by Thomas of Ercildoun, also know as Thomas the Rhymer.

An historical figure born around 1220, he had the reputation of a wizard and is still known for his prophecies. After the Jedburgh manifestation he predicted that a troubled time for Scotland would commence on 16 March of the following year.

On that day King Alexander died without having sired an heir. And the riddle has remained down the years – who or what was the sinister figure that had materialised so briefly at the royal wedding feast.

Visiting Information

Now a museum, it is situated at Jedburgh, Roxburghshire, on the A68.

LOWTHER CASTLE

The phantom coach of Lowther Castle goes back to the extraordinary Sir James Lowther, 1st Lord Lonsdale. The castle was certainly a grand setting for paranormal activity. A guidebook published at the beginning of the last century described it thus:

> ... situated in a beautiful timbered park, comprising several hundred acres, where a herd of red deer roam, and in the rutting season stags make the place resound with their bellowing. The castle, a magnificent Windsor of the north, stands in palatial splendour, with its numerous towers, terraces and battlements, impressing the beholder with the dignity and importance of the Lowther family.

The Lowther family was said to have settled in Westmorland generations before William the Conqueror settled in England, the name being derived from the Danish words 'louth' and 'er' which signify fortune and honour. Certainly the family has lived up to its name; ever since the twelfth century, when the area was annexed to the English Crown, there has been a Lowther of Lowther. Through the centuries the Lowthers added to their property until they became 'equal to princes in social position, frequently entertaining monarchs as their guests'.

Thomas de Quincey, famous for his *Confessions of an English Opium-Eater*, and who lived for some time in the Lake District where he was friendly with Wordsworth, wrote of Sir James Lowther, the first Lord Lonsdale:

> He was a true feudal chieftain, and in the very approaches to his mansion, in the style of his equipage, or whatever else he was likely to meet the public eye, he delighted to express his disdain of modern by the haughty carelessness of his magnificence. The coach in which he used to visit was old and neglected, his horses were fine and untrained and such was the impression diffused about him by his gloomy temper and habits of oppression that, according to the declaration of a Penrith contemporary of the old

Lowther Castle.

despot, the streets were silent as he traversed them, and an awe sat upon many faces ... Superstition made his 'ghost' more terrible and notorious after his death than the veritable 'despot' had been during his life.

The eccentric noble, who surrounded his castle with herds of wild horses and revelled in its gloomy woods, had a weak spot. He fell desperately in love with a young woman who, in those days, was described as having 'no connection'. He persuaded her to live with him and, leaving his residence to the wild horses, set up home in a splendid Hampshire house where a whole army of servants was engaged to serve her.

Despite the beautiful home and riches, the girl did not find the happiness she expected. It is doubtful if she actually loved the moody lord, rather she was awed by the rank and wealth.

The final act of the tragedy for Sir James came when his beloved mistress was taken ill and died. His grief was such that none of the servants dared mention the fact that death had claimed her. The earl left her body on her bed, and such was his domineering character and obsession that even the butler, as the foremost servant, was too terrified to suggest that the corpse should be interred. At last sanity must have returned to Sir James for he made arrangements for the body to be buried at a cemetery in Paddington, London. Even this was no straightforward operation. He ordered a detachment of the Cumberland militia to be sent down to the capital to mount guard night and day at the cemetery until the tomb was finished. After the funeral took place the earl wore deep mourning for the rest of his life.

With such a strange character it was almost to be expected that after his death his spirit would be restless and return to haunt Lowther Castle.

The manifestations began at his funeral. When the pall-bearers lifted the coffin it seemed to be possessed by some supernatural power which made it sway so alarmingly that only with great difficulty it was carried to the graveside.

A certain Mr Sullivan, who had a reputation for 'keeping records', and who was present at the grotesque ceremony, wrote: 'He was with difficulty buried ... the power of creating alarm was not interred with his bones. There were disturbances in the hall, noises in the stables; neither men nor animals were suffered to rest ...'

The ghostly earl did not restrict himself to poltergeist activity within Lowther Castle. At night his coach – now an unearthly vehicle – which had caused such awe in the streets of Penrith, was sometimes glimpsed racing silently along the roads near to the castle.

Although the spectral coach was often observed and feared, the phantom of Sir James was never seen, although he made his presence felt through continual disturbances in the castle.

Finally the supernatural activity became too much for the inhabitants of the castle and an exorcism was arranged. According to an old account 'after many an effort the priest *laid* him under a large rock called Wallow Crag, and laid him forever'.

Visiting Information

Situated just south of Lowther village about 4 miles from Penrith, Cumbria. On private land.

LUDLOW CASTLE

It was a siege that led to the haunting of Ludlow Castle. Built after the Norman Conquest, it was one of the thirty-two castles set up to guard the Welsh Marches. During the reign of Henry II there was much bitter fighting in the border area and frequently the castle's garrison rode out to defend the nearby town against Welsh raiders.

On one such occasion the castle was left with only a few soldiers to guard it. It gave a girl, by the name of Marion de la Bryere, the opportunity to lower a rope from the castle wall as her lover had requested so he could climb it and keep a tryst with her.

When he reached the battlements and embraced her she was so delighted that she forgot the rope and it was left dangling to the ground below. The suitor led her a little distance away and for a while she lay happily in his arms.

Suddenly a sound made Marion look up to see another figure appear over the battlements followed by another and another. She realised she had been betrayed and, almost demented at how she had been so cynically exploited by her lover, pulled the dagger from his belt and ran the blade into his heart. Then she ran to the top of the Hanging Tower and leapt into space to die on the rocks below. More ropes were added to Marion's by the invaders, over a hundred men scaled the castle wall and soon it was under their control.

Before long stories began to spread that Marion's white form had been seen re-enacting the drama she had played out on the Hanging Tower, a drama which for centuries has denied her spirit rest.

Another paranormal phenomenon which dates back to the tragedy is a strange rasping sound heard close to the Hanging Tower. It is thought to be the death rattle of the young man who deceived Marion and died at her hand. Although the White Lady of Ludlow Castle has not been glimpsed in recent years, there have been reports of this sinister sound.

Visiting Information

Situated in Ludlow, Shropshire. Open daily February to November, weekends only December to January.

LYMPNE CASTLE

Lympne Castle is haunted by one of Britain's oldest ghosts. It is not surprising the site of this interesting castle goes back into Roman, Saxon and Norman history. It was built on the site of a Roman watch-tower which overlooked an ancient Roman shore fort known as Stutfall Castle. Its position gave it advantageous views over the Romney Marshes and across the Channel to France. The building was restored in 1905.

The castle ghost is that of a Roman soldier who is heard climbing up the stairs in the East Tower. It is surmised that he accidentally fell to his death because, while his footsteps sound on the steps as he goes up, they are never heard coming down.

Ancient history was also the background to the six ghostly shapes which have been glimpsed within the castle walls. They are linked to the tradition that six fugitive Saxons were slain there by Norman soldiers after the Conquest.

Visiting Information

Situated at Lympne, Kent. Not open to the public.

MEGGERNIE CASTLE

Meggernie Castle was built in 1580 by 'Mad Colin' Campbell who earned his nickname for the daring abduction of the Countess of Erroll. Later it passed into the hands of the Menzies clan, and it is the ghostly victim of one of these lairds that has kissed guests there with bitter lips.

One account of the apparition, which appears only from the waist up, was written in 1862 after a Mr E.J. Simons, of Ullesthorpe, visited the castle for a house party. Here he met an old friend named Beaumont Fetherstone. Their adjoining rooms were situated in the castle tower, giving them a view of the River Lyon. Simons saw a door in the wall of his room and thought it opened into his friend's room. He tried to open it but found it was sealed.

Fetherstone said that in his room there was a similar door which he thought opened into a closet built in the massive wall between their rooms but it too was sealed. Unable to open the doors, they went to bed. Sometime after midnight Simons was awakened by what seemed like a feverish kiss on his cheek, so hot that it made him wince.

He jumped out of bed and then to his horror saw the upper half of a woman gliding towards the sealed door through which she disappeared. After a moment he summoned up enough courage to follow her, but when he reached the connecting door he found it just as securely fastened as when he and Fetherstone had examined it. Next he went to a mirror, expecting to see a burn mark on his face but, despite the fact that he could still feel the unearthly imprint, there was not a mark to be seen.

Early next morning he sought out Fetherstone and told him about the ghostly visitation. Fetherstone said he'd had a similar experience. The two shaken men decided to get a third party to hear their stories dispassionately and compare them. The result was that both were removed from the tower.

Fetherstone was so impressed by his own experience that he wrote a description of it which was later published in A.A. MacGregor's book *Phantom Footsteps*:

At Meggernie Castle, Perthshire, 2 a.m. I was awakened by a pink light in the room, and saw a female at the foot of the bed. At first

I took her for a housekeeper walking in her sleep. She came along the side of the bed and bent over me. I raised myself, and she retreated and went into a small room made out of the thickness of the wall, opposite the foot of the bed.

He concluded, 'The phantom seemed minus legs which I am glad to say I did not realise at the first glimpse or I should have been in an even greater funk than I was.'

The explanation for the appearance of the mutilated spectre goes back to when one of the chiefs of the Menzies Clan resided in the castle. By nature he was a man who found it impossible to curb his obsessive jealousy. One day it reached a pitch of such paranoia that he murdered his attractive young wife high in the castle tower. When sanity returned he devised a plan to escape retribution.

His first act was to cleave the corpse in two so he could hide it in a chest standing in the closet built into the wall of the tower. He then announced that he and his wife had decided to travel abroad and, during the night, he departed without the servants seeing them off.

Some months later he returned to Meggernie and said that his wife had drowned while on holiday. He then retired to the tower where he unsealed the closet with its hideous secret. When the rest of the castle slept he took the lower half of the corpse from the chest and carried it down the tower stairs and out to a nearby churchyard where he buried it.

It seems that the next night he was going to bury the rest of the body. Instead it was his body that was found in the tower. He had been murdered by an unknown assailant, most likely some person who guessed the true cause of the lady's disappearance and avenged her.

Visiting Information

Situated halfway along Glen Lyon close to Aberfeldy, Perthshire. Check website for information.

1   Bamburgh Castle – legend tells it was once Sir Lancelot's castle 'Joyous Garde'.

2   Alnwick Castle – a fine setting for a vampire visitation and *Harry Potter*.

6   Prudhoe Castle – haunted by a mysterious 'Grey Lady'.

7   Dunstaffnage Castle – home of a fairy woman known as Elle Maid who befriended the family.

8   Windsor Castle – the castle's Long Walk, once haunted by the ghost of a Grenadier.

9   Dunstanburgh Castle – a sleeping beauty and entranced warriors.

10   Featherstone Castle – a wedding feast with phantom guests.

11   Greystoke Castle – a vanishing guest and a noisy monk.

12   Dacre Castle – three royal ghosts.

13   Hermitage Castle – Sir Walter Scott's favourite castle despite its 'load of iniquity'.

14   Caister Castle – a harbinger of death in the form of a phantom coach.

MOY CASTLE

A feud which erupted between a son and his father led to the periodic return of a headless horseman. This spectral rider has been seen riding between Loch Squabain and Moy Castle whose square ruins once guarded Loch Buie in the south of the Island of Mull. The son's name was Ewan and his father was the MacLaine chief who held Moy in the early part of the sixteenth century.

Having married an extremely ambitious wife, Ewan decided it was best to leave his father's castle and set up an establishment of his own on a tiny island in Loch Squabain, once the site of a prehistoric fortification.

Ewan's wife was far from satisfied when she compared her husband's small fortress with the far more spacious and splendid Moy Castle. Her displeasure had such an effect on Ewan that he began complaining to his father that he was not adequately housed for a man of his station and something must be done about it. In response MacLaine would shrug and tell his son to be patient; one day he would inherit Moy but until then he should be satisfied with what he had. Ewan's discontent, cunningly fanned by his wife, intensified until an open quarrel flared between the chief and his son. The former bitterly resented the way his heir hungered for his inheritance, the latter full of complaint that his father was not providing properly for him.

Tension mounted between MacLaine and his clansmen and Ewan and his partisans. Finally fighting broke out between the opposing adherents, thus starting one of those blood feuds which were the bane of Scotland. MacLaine was so angered by this that he planned to lead a raiding party to Loch Squabain.

Just prior to this, as Ewan was walking towards the shore of the loch he saw an old woman bending over a brook washing shirts. Ewan must have felt his blood chill because she was a dreaded Bean-nighe. One of the most dismal characters in folklore, the Bean-nighe was an unearthly washing woman who was sometimes seen washing the clothes of those about to die in battle.

The Bean-nighe of Mull was believed to have exceptionally long breasts, so long in fact that as she bent over her ill-omened work she would push them back over her shoulders. When a man beheld her at work the correct procedure was to steal up behind her unawares, seize one of her pendulous breasts and declare that she was his foster mother.

Then the Bean-nighe would answer any question that he asked, the obvious one being whose linen was she washing. If it belonged to an enemy she would continue her work, but if the washing were that of her new foster son she could be prevailed upon to stop.

In the case of Ewan it would seem he was too late to halt the Bean-nighe's fateful work but she did have a crumb of comfort for him. She explained that although his shirt was among those of the men destined to die, he might be spared if on the following morning his wife gave him a generous lump of butter at breakfast without him having to ask to do so.

One can imagine the state of Ewan's feelings the next day when he sat at table and waited for his wife to give him his food. As one might imagine she had little interest in domestic matters and told her husband he would have to eat his bread dry as they had run out of butter.

Knowing that there was no way of escaping his weird fate, Ewan led his men from Loch Squabain to meet his father's raiding party. In the fighting his head was struck from his shoulders – a lesson to all sons who would marry thriftless wives and quarrel with their fathers.

Visiting Information

The ruined remains of the castle are to be seen by Loch Buie, Isle of Mull.

MUNCASTER CASTLE

uncaster Castle goes far back into history. Originally a pele tower built on Roman foundations, it has been added to down the centuries and in 1862 gained its present shape when rebuilding was done under the direction of the famous architect Anthony Salvin. The castle has a famous talisman known as the 'Luck of Muncaster', which must be effective as it has been the home of the Pennington family since 1208. The Luck is a bowl of green-tinted glass, decorated with purple and gold, and is most likely Venetian in origin. It was presented to the Penningtons in 1464 by Henry VI in appreciation of the hospitality accorded him when he was a fugitive after being deposed in the Wars of the Roses.

A couplet associated with the the bowl states:

> In Muncaster Castle good luck shall be
> Till this charmed cup is broken.

The castle has two ghosts. One is of the luckless King Henry, who died under suspicious circumstances in the Tower of London after his rival Edward IV's victory at the battle of Tewkesbury. His phantom has appeared in the chamber he used when he was given shelter in the castle.

The other ghost is headless. Legend tells he was a young carpenter who forgot his proper station in life when he fell in love with Helwise, the daughter of Sir Ferdinand Pennington. It would have been better for the youth if the girl had not returned his feelings but she did, infuriating her father who had already arranged her marriage with a suitable knight.

Sir Ferdinand paid his jester to assassinate the young carpenter. In order to prove he had done the deed the jester cut off his victim's head and showed it to his master. Since then the luckless suitor's phantom has appeared in his mutilated condition as a mute reminder of the crime.

Visiting Information

Situated to the south of Ravenglass, Cumbria. Open daily.

NAWORTH CASTLE

K nown as the White Lady of Naworth, the ghost of a beautiful girl has haunted the castle as the consequence of a tragedy long ago.

Steeped in history, the castle was at one time the great Border stronghold of Lord Wardens of the Marches. It goes back to 1336 when Ranulph de Dacre, Earl of Cumberland, was granted a licence to crenellate his home, though experts say the present castle dates from 1585.

Until the middle of the nineteenth century it was considered to be one of the most perfect feudal fortresses of the Border, one of the 'Lions of the North'. Then a fire destroyed most of its woodwork and damaged the structure. Thanks to restoration by the 6th Earl of Carlisle it regained its original appearance.

Old Border ballads refer to 'Naworth's iron towers', and these are still to be seen, the east tower being Lord Howard's Tower and the west Dacre's Tower, thus incorporating the names of the two great families who in turn resided in it for over seven centuries.

Naworth was held by the Dacre family until 1577, when it was inherited by Lady Elizabeth Dacre who, when she was fourteen, married Lord William Howard who was less than a year her senior. He was to grow into the famous Belted Will, one of the Border's renowned characters.

According to Sir Walter Scott he earned the nickname because

> His Bilboa blade, by marchmen felt,
> Hung in a broad and studded belt,
> Hence, in rude phrase, the Borderers still,
> Call noble Howard, 'Belted Will'.

The event which gave rising to the haunting of Naworth took place some years before Belted Will became warden. According to the tradition, Lord Dacre of Naworth had an affair with a beautiful but lowborn girl. He did not tell her of his aristocratic background and unaware of his true name, she gladly gave her heart and body to him, fondly believing when she found herself pregnant that he would make an honest woman of her.

Naworth Castle.

It was then, in the tradition of deceived maidens, that he told her of his rank and added he could not marry her because a marriage had already been arranged with a woman of his station. After the distraught girl gave birth to a son she drowned herself in the stream by the castle on the day her false lover was married.

The next morning Lord Dacre walked out with his new wife and found the girl in the water, her hair streaming about her like Ophelia's. At the same time the girl's mother, who had been searching desperately for her daughter through the night, came upon the scene. Blaming Lord Dacre for her daughter's tragedy, she cried out a curse which is remembered in an ancient rhyme.

O curst be the cruel hand
That wrought this hour to me!
May evil grim aye follow him
Until the day he dee.

Lord Dacre did not live very long after that. Three years after his death, in 1577, his only legitimate son fell from a rocking horse so that, according to a chronicler, 'he had the brains bruised out of his head'.

The male line of the Dacres died out, and the castle passed to Belted Will, through his marriage to Lady Elizabeth, proving to the satisfaction of the local folk the effectiveness of curses. But though the White Lady had her revenge her spirit remained restless.

Visiting Information

Situated close to the River Irthing west of Greenhead, Northumberland. Visits by appointment only.

POWIS CASTLE

Over two centuries ago Powis Castle was the scene of a cruel trick played on a simple spinning woman who – thanks to the appearance of a mysterious ghost – had the last laugh.

And the incident is one of the best recorded castle hauntings.

Known locally as the Red Castle because of the ruddy colour of its sandstone walls, Powis Castle was enlarged from an earlier fortification by Gruffydd Baron de la Pole, a supported of Edward I who conquered Wales.

When the family died out in the middle of the sixteenth century it was bought by Sir Edward Herbert. During the Civil War it was captured by the Parliamentarians and after the Restoration it was returned to the Herberts.

In 1780 there was a lot of gossip about a woman who had seen the castle's ghost which was supposed to have revealed a secret to her. A preacher named John Hampson, who was held in high esteem by the Wesleyan Methodists, was curious about the story and interviewed the woman who vowed that the story was true and that there were many witnesses who would vouch for it.

She explained to Mr Hampson, who made notes, that she was a spinster in both meanings of the word – she was unmarried and earned her living by spinning. As farmers in the district grew their own flax she went to their farmhouses where she spun it on the spot. On one occasion, when her usual customers had no work for her, she decided to try her luck at the castle.

When she arrived at the gloomy fortress she was told by the steward that the Earl of Powis and his family were away and he could not say if a spinner was required. But his wife, who seems to have had a cruel streak in her nature, found some sewing work for the woman, saying that she could stay at the castle and earn her keep until the earl returned.

What surprised and delighted the spinner was the luxurious room she was allotted and could hardly believe a person as humble as she should be allowed to sleep there. What she did not know was that it was the castle's haunted room, and the steward's wife, encouraged by the rest of the servants, had placed her there to see what would happen.

They bade her good night and the poor spinner may have wondered why they locked the door but perhaps she thought this was the usual practice in great castles, a safeguard against strangers being tempted to take some of the family silver.

Before going to bed she sat by the fire to read her Bible. After a while she looked up to see a man had silently entered the room wearing a 'gold-lace suit and hat'. Although she was rather surprised she was not then afraid, thinking perhaps that he was some superior servant who had come to make sure everything was in order.

The figure walked across to a corner window and stood still, giving the impression that he expected her to say something. She was tongue-tied and the mysterious visitor walked back to the doorway and passed through it. The bewildered woman suddenly realised that he had entered and left without the sound of the lock grating. The silence of his entry and leaving made her realise he must be a phantom.

Everything fell into place. She was cruelly imprisoned in order to be haunted. All she could think to do was pray and she knelt beside her bed. Then she looked up to see the finely dressed apparition had returned and again it seemed that he expected her to speak.

She summoned up all her courage and asked, 'Pray sir, who are you?'

'Take up the candle and follow me and I shall tell you,' was the reply.

In telling her story to Mr Hampson, she described walking along a seemingly endless corridor and then into a small room. She said, 'As the room was small and as I believed him to be a spirit, I stopped at the door. He turned and said, "Walk in, I will not hurt you." So I walked in.

'He said, "Observe what I do." He stooped and lifted one of the floor boards, and in the cavity beneath was a box with an iron handle.

'He said, "Do you see that box?"

'I said, "Yes I do."

'Then he stepped to one side of the room and showed me a crevice in the wall, where he said a key was hid that would open it.

'He said, "This box and key must be taken out and sent to the Earl in London. Will you see it done?"

'I said, "I will do my best to get it done."

'He said, "Do – and I will trouble the house no more."

'Then he left me. I stepped to the room door and set up a shout. The steward and his wife, with the other servants, came to me immediately. It seemed they had all been waiting to see the issue of the interview betwixt me and the apparition.

'I told them the story and showed them the box. The steward dared not meddle with it but his wife had more courage and found the key.'

The spinner said that the chest was heavy but she did not see it opened and therefore could not see what was in it. The steward dispatched the box to his master in London with a letter describing the curious way it had been found. By return came a letter ordering the steward to tell the spinner that if she wished she could reside in the castle for the rest of her life, or if she wished to remain in her cottage she would be well provided for. She accepted the latter offer, being grateful to the earl and the ghost. But neither she nor Mr Hampson ever heard an explanation for the apparition or got a hint of what was contained in the hidden chest.

Visiting Information

Situated less than a mile south of Welshpool, Shropshire. Open daily April to November apart from Tuesdays.

PRUDHOE CASTLE

The history of Prudhoe Castle has been turbulent at times so it is not surprising that it has a resident ghost. The castle was built on a cliff which rose 60ft above the Tyne. The river acted as part of the defences while a fosse was dug so that the castle could only be entered by means of a drawbridge. Since Prudhoe was begun in the twelfth century the river has altered its course but the castle is still awesome, and the remains of its 75ft-high keep live up to the name which meant 'proud height'.

In 1173 the Scots unsportingly attacked it before it was completed. A year later another attack was mounted, also led by William the Lyon of Scotland, who had a vendetta with Odinel d'Umfraville who held the castle. The Scottish king had vowed, 'May I be accursed, excommunicated by a priest, put to shame and discomfited if I give the castle of Odinel a fixed time or respite ...'

Prudhoe Castle.

Prudhoe Castle.

Odinel fled his besieged castle and rode south to raise forces which finally engaged William the Lyon at Alnwick on 13 June 1174. The result was that William was captured by the Lord of Prudhoe and was only liberated after he performed homage for his kingdom to Henry II of England.

In 1381 Gilbert d'Umfraville died, the last of his line. As his widow Maud was a Percy, Prudhoe Castle passed into the hands of that famous Border family who were a law unto themselves and fell foul of Henry IV. The king personally led a huge army to capture the castle. But by 1557 it was back in Percy ownership, though it was to continue to have its dramas.

Thomas Percy, who was involved in the Gunpowder Plot, was suspected of hiding there and Oliver Cromwell, whose dislike of castles was well known, ordered cannon to fire at its tower.

The castle ghost, who has walked its passages by night, is known as the Grey Lady. She may be re-enacting some forgotten drama. Her story might have a connection with the secret tunnel which was once supposed to connect Prudhoe with Bywell Castle several miles to the west. But her identity, and the reason for her castle-bound state, seem to have been forgotten in the mists of time.

Visiting Information

Overlooking the River Tyne, the castle is situated just north of Prudhoe, Northumberland. Open March to September except on Tuesdays and Wednesdays.

RAIT CASTLE

ait Castle is haunted by a phantom woman in a dress dyed with blood that was spilled in the year 1524. At that time the castle was held by the Comyns Clan who were involved in a feud with the MacKintoshes.

Pretending they wished peace, the Comyns invited their enemies to Rait for a feast of reconciliation, though they secretly planned to massacre them as they sat in the banqueting hall. The MacKintoshes accepted the invitation but, highly suspicious of the gesture, they came heavily armed.

Seeing his guests approach as though ready for battle, the chief of the Comyns believed that his daughter had betrayed his treacherous plan on account of the love she felt for a young MacKintosh – a Romeo and Juliet situation. In his fury the chief had his daughter's hands lopped off.

As she saw her blood staining her dress the girl leaped to her death from the top of the castle, but retribution caught up with her cruel father when he and his followers were slaughtered by Mackintosh clansmen at nearby Balbair. From then on the castle was abandoned though a stop was made there by 'Butcher' Cumberland with his army before vanquishing the Jacobites at Culloden in 1746.

Now only occasional glimpses of the phantom girl in the ruin remain as a mute testimony to the bitterness of clan warfare.

Visiting Information

The castle is situated 3 miles south of Nairn in Nairnshire. Not open to the public. Permission required to visit.

ROCHESTER CASTLE

A young woman, her body transfixed by an arrow, is the spectre at Rochester Castle which is still believed to appear after seven centuries. The name of the distraught ghost was Lady Blanche de Warrene, and she was betrothed to Ralph de Capo, the lord of Rochester Castle, whose mighty ruins dominate the Medway as they have done for a thousand years.

The first castle was built on the site of a Roman camp by Bishop Gundulf, known as The Good, in 1080 and was the original example of the square Norman keep built in England. It was first besieged by King John in 1215 when over a hundred rebel knights defied him; for twelve weeks five powerful catapults hurled massive stones against its walls while bands of archers kept up a hail of arrows whistling over its crenellated ramparts.

It was not until the king ordered miners to undermine the south-west tower that the royal forces managed to get within the outer walls though the defenders retained the keep until starvation forced them to surrender.

The following year the castle was held by the French after the Dauphin Louis captured Rochester on behalf of the barons. But when King John died, rumour says of poison after losing his treasure in the Wash, the Dauphin's forces returned to France and the castle had a brief period of peace. This lasted until 1264, when it was besieged by Simon de Montfort. Then tragedy overtook Lady Blanche, with the result her restless shade still walks the ancient battlements.

Ralph de Capo who, having proved himself as a crusader, now bitterly resisted de Montfort's army. Serving under de Montfort was Sir Gilbert de Clare who had a particular desire to see the castle fall as his suit had been rejected by Lady Blanche.

Simon de Montfort was less successful in besieging the Rochester than King John and finally he raised the siege. As the army was leaving Sir Ralph and his knights sallied forth from the castle to harry the retreating foe. During the confusion Sir Gilbert de Clare donned a surcoat which had the same emblem worked in it as that worn by Sir Ralph. Thus disguised, he boldly rode to the now undefended castle and climbed to the battlements where Lady Blanche had watched the distant foray.

Rochester
Castle. (stock.
xchng)

Suddenly she turned to see Sir Gilbert, and she knew he was thirsting for revenge for the slight she had given him before the siege. She fled along the top of the castle wall which still rises 113ft above the ground to seek sanctuary in the Round Tower. Here she barricaded the door and climbed the circular staircase to the top. Sir Gilbert's battle-axe soon smashed the door and Lady Blanche knew her choice lay between submitting to the brutal knight or leaping from the highest castle in the country.

Meanwhile Sir Ralph de Capo was returning at the head of his cavalry, but as he looked up at his castle he saw two struggling figures silhouetted on the top of the Round Tower.

Realising that Lady Blanche was being molested he leapt from the saddle, seized a bow from an archer and loosed an arrow. It flew to the top of the tower and struck his enemy's armour which deflected the arrow straight into the heart of Lady Blanche. She fell to the stone flags of the tower with the bitter knowledge that her lover had accidentally ended her life. It is not known what fate overtook Sir Gilbert St Clare but one can be sure he paid for his crime. And it was recorded that on the same night as she died, Lady Blanche's ghost was seen moving along the castle walls, weeping at her cruel destiny.

Another ghost associated with Rochester Castle is that of Charles Dickens. Before his death he expressed the wish to be buried in the St Nicholas' church graveyard by the castle. His wishes were ignored and he was interred in Westminster Abbey. Since then there have been accounts of a spectre, with features remarkably like those of Dickens, wandering among the tombstones of the old burial ground.

Visiting Information

Situated on the east bank of the Medway in Rochester, Kent. Open daily.

ROSLIN CASTLE

A highly dramatic portent preceded the deaths of the lords of Roslin Castle, which was built in the fourteenth century by Sir William St Clair. His descendant William, Prince of Orkney, began the nearby Roslin Chapel which happily has not decayed like the castle. It is a gem of British medieval architecture and it is this ornate building that portended the deaths of the St Clairs, and later those of the Erskines who took over the property when the St Clairs died out in 1778. The forewarning took the form of the chapel appearing to be on fire with phantom flames that left no scorch marks on its extraordinary carved stonework and grotesque gargoyles. Sir Walter Scott, that ardent collector of traditional tales, wrote thus of the phenomenon in his long poem *The Lay of the Last Minstrel:*

> Seem'd all on fire, within, around,
> Deep sacristy and altar's pale;
> Shone every pillar foliage-bound,
> And glimmer'd all the dead men's mail.
> Blazed battlement and pinnet high,
> Blazed every rose-carved buttress fair;
> So still they blaze, when fate is nigh
> The lordly line of Hugh St Clair.

There is no traditional explanation of Roslin's strange portending but another supernatural story connected with the Roslin chapel has well-known origins. It relates to one of the fourteen beautifully carved columns in the chapel known as the Apprentice Pillar which supports an intricately sculpted arch. The amazing detail of the pillar includes tiny figures of angels playing musical instruments.

When the pillar was being sculpted it was regarded as the finest example of stone carving but the chief stone mason was so dedicated to the work that he felt he could not complete it satisfactorily without further study of his craft. He went away to perfect his skill under a famous sculptor and while he was away a young apprentice innocently worked on the pillar. He had just completed it when his master returned.

Roslin Castle.

Despite the fact that the young man's work was perfect the mason was so furious he had not completed the work himself that he struck the apprentice on the head with a mallet, killing him on the spot. After the tragedy there was widespread local belief that the chapel was haunted by the shade of the apprentice returning to what had been his masterpiece in life.

Another aspect of the chapel is its past connection with the Knights Templar. Links between the Templars and the St Clair family were very strong and there is conjecture that secrets of the order may have been incorporated in the chapel's fantastical stonework and pillars. There was also a Masonic connection with the chapel which attracts many visitors today.

Visiting Information

Nine miles south of Edinburgh, the castle is situated at Roslin, Midlothian. On private land, the castle is not open to the public but the nearby Roslin Chapel is open daily.

SCOTNEY CASTLE

A journalist once wrote that on a fine English summer's day there is no more beautiful sight than that of Scotney Castle dreaming above its haunted moat. It was also the setting for a long-ago mystery.

It was built in the fourteenth century by Roger Ashburnham. Later it passed into the hands of the ardent Catholic Darrell family who constructed secret hiding places to shelter priests after England's break with Rome. The most famous episode connected with these was when Jesuit 'missionary' Father Blount hid in one while the castle was occupied by the Darrells' enemies. Twice he was nearly captured during his seven-year stay.

The mystery connected with Scotney occurred on 12 December 1720, at the funeral of Arthur Darrell who had died while on the Continent. When the coffin was lowered into the grave a stranger swathed in a black cloak was watching the ceremony. As clods of earth began to thud on the coffin lid the unknown spectator muttered, 'It is me they think they are burying!'

After this curious remark he vanished. According to some accounts, he disappeared before the mourners' eyes.

Was it the ghost of Arthur Darrell or did he have a secret reason for wishing to be thought dead? A sexton named John Bailey, who died in 1867, claimed that when he was preparing a grave in the Scotney Chapel of Lamberhurst church he unexpectedly came upon a timeworn iron-studded coffin. Prising off the lid to try and find out whom it contained he was amazed to see that it was full of stones.

There was no name on the coffin and it was thought that it might be Arthur Darrell's. The unsolved question was that if for some secret reason he had wished to be thought of as dead why did he risk detection by attending his own funeral?

Scotney's resident ghost appears as a figure crawling painfully from the moat. The eerie phenomenon is glimpsed only on dark nights. He was an excise officer who was murdered by a gang of smugglers on a moonless night when he surprised them with a pack train of contraband.

His body was thrown into Scotney's moat. Now in his ghostly form, he materialises in the water and, festooned with water-weed,

Scotney Castle.

he struggles up the bank and makes his way to the door of the castle before dissolving and leaving a dank miasma behind.

Visiting Information

Situated a mile south-east of Lamberhurst, Kent. The house and gardens are open Wednesdays to Sundays 15 February to 3 November. Weekends only 3 November to 23 December.

SHERBORNE CASTLE

Sherborne Castle has been the haunting ground of one England's most distinguished ghosts, and at one stage of its long history it had a holy curse laid upon it.

After the Norman Conquest Osmund, later the Bishop of Sarum, was given the site and in 1102 the castle was completed. Later in the reign of Edward III there was a complicated dispute over the ownership of the castle which became so heated that the then Bishop of Sarum put on armour and challenged the Earl of Salisbury to combat in order to decide the question.

The matter was finally decided without violence, but in order to ensure the Church's rights to it in the future a holy curse was invoked on anyone who should try to wrest it from the bishopric.

The imprecation seems to have been effective. After Sherborne Castle ceased to be Church property, some of its unlucky owners, including the Earl of Somerset, met with tragic fates. In 1592 Elizabeth I leased it to Sir Walter Raleigh. As the cost of restoring it became increasingly heavy Sir Walter decided to spend his money on a new residence by the castle. This he began in 1594, referring to it as The Lodge. Then, after falling from royal favour, he was confined to the Tower of London where he was finally executed in 1618.

On St Michael's Eve the spectre of Sir Walter returns to the old garden of Sherborne Castle, where, having done his annual walk, he dematerialises in the arbour by an oak tree named after him.

Visiting Information

Situated just east of Sherborne, Dorset. Open daily apart from Mondays and Fridays 28 March to 28 October.

SPEDLIN'S TOWER

The legend behind Spedlin's Tower's haunting – similar to that of Haughton Castle – goes back to the Restoration when Sir Alexander Jardine had a miller named Porteas arrested on the charge of trying to burn down his own mill. The reason for his strange behaviour is not recorded but it was strong enough for the miller to be imprisoned in a dungeon beneath the tower.

Soon afterwards Sir Alexander received a message requiring him to go to Edinburgh. It was some time after he had reached the city and was passing the city prison that he realised that he was carrying the only key to the Spedlin dungeon in his pocket.

He sent a messenger galloping back to the tower with the key, but in the meantime the miller had died of starvation. But if the heavy locked door of the dungeon had been too thick for Porteous's cries to reach the inhabitants of the castle, it was no barrier for his ghost. Day and night he revenged himself on the Jardines with every conceivable poltergeist trick.

Finally it was a service of exorcism that drove the frantic spirit back into the dungeon, and a Bible which had been used in the service was placed in the stairwell leading down to the cell to keep Porteas from returning to plague the family.

The Bible could not muffle the dead miller's voice and often a scream would ring through the tower followed by the words, 'Let me out, let me out. I am dying of hunger!'

Sometimes someone more daring than the rest would creep down the stairs and by putting his ear to the iron-studded door hear the sounds of Porteous cursing the family and the scrabbling of his fingers. If a twig was pushed through the keyhole its bark would have been chewed.

In the course of time the Jardine family moved to a new mansion, known as Jardine Hall, but the Bible was left in its niche to contain the angry spirit.

Visiting Information
Situated on the south-west bank of the River Annan, Dumfrieshire.

ST DONAT'S CASTLE

S t Donat's has the reputation of being one of the most haunted castles in Wales. The building goes back to the beginning of the fourteenth century and has been added to from time to time. Today it accommodates Atlantic College, an international sixth form college which, founded in 1962, was the first of twelve United World Colleges.

At the beginning of the last century there was an alarming outbreak of paranormal activity. The most extraordinary aspect of this manifestation was a spectral panther which prowled silently along the castle corridors. As with much psychical phenomena, there is no known explanation as to why such an exotic manifestation should haunt a Welsh castle.

Other occurrences that alarmed the owners and staff of St Donat's included a mysterious light which glowed in one of the bedrooms 'having the semblance of a large staring eye, a witch-like wraith frequently glimpsed in the armoury, and an invisible pianist who produced chords from a piano even when the lid was locked in place.

Such was the distress this activity caused the then owner that he advertised the castle for sale. But before he received any offers, he heard of a faith-healer who also specialised in exorcism, and he wrote to him asking for help.

When the faith-healer arrived at the castle he listened to a recital of the hauntings and then, having asked the owner to sit in the hall with the main door wide open, retired to the room where the strange eye-like light shone. Here he prayed and concentrated on dispelling the spectres. Suddenly a great gust of wind swirled about him, blew down the staircase and through the hall, practically toppling the owner, and out through the open doorway.

St Donat's baronial hall was constructed in the sixteenth century on the site of a castle built a couple of centuries earlier by Guillaume le Esterling, the ancestor of the Stradling family who held the castle until the middle of the eighteenth century. Then the heir of the castle planned to make the Grand Tour in the company of a young man named Tyrrwhit, and before setting out the two friends signed a pact that if either died the property of the deceased would be bequeathed to the other.

St Donat's Castle.

While they were in France news reached them that Stradling's father had died and so his son inherited the castle. He did not have long to enjoy his inheritance as shortly afterwards he was killed in a duel at Montpelier. Tyrrwhit then claimed the castle according to the agreement.

Believing the duel had been engineered to remove the heir, the Stradlings fought the claim, and it was only after a long period of litigation that Tyrrwhit was able to gain the property. Some generations later the castle was bought back by a descendant of the Stradlings.

The unfortunate Stradling heir was not the only member of the family to die violently. According to tradition, a Lady Stradling was done to death by a member of the family, and since then her ghost has appeared at intervals at St Donat's. Wirt Sykes wrote in his book *British Goblins* that the beautiful shade of the murdered lady appeared 'when any mishap is about to fall on a member of the house of Stradling ... She wears high-heeled shoes, and a long trailing gown.'

The howling of dogs in the neighbourhood accompanies the appearance of her ghost which walks either in the castle or its grounds.

Visiting Information

Looking out over the Bristol Channel, the castle stands in St Donats village close to Llantwit, Glamorganshire. Not open to the public.

TAUNTON CASTLE

Taunton Castle is the scene of several paranormal manifestations and poltergeist activity going back to the Monmouth Rebellion which left such a tragic shadow over the West Country. Built on the site of a Saxon earthwork fortification in the twelfth century, the castle now houses the Taunton Museum and the Castle Hotel. In the so-called Fiddler's Room the unearthly strains of a fiddle have sounded while in the museum section visitors have heard a mysterious tramping noise as though invisible soldiers were passing through. Other castle ghosts are visible.

On 20 June 1685, the Duke of Monmouth, the natural son of Charles II and Lucy Walter, was proclaimed James II by his Protestant adherents at Taunton. That night his lieutenants celebrated the occasion with a revel at the castle. Ladies, faithful to the pretender's cause, danced with the officers who called for madder music and stronger wine. It was the last time they were to celebrate because a few days later the duke attempted to surprise a 2,700-strong royal army on Sedgemoor. Although his peasant force was just a hundred less than that number it stood little chance against professional soldiers and their artillery. Cannons cut ghastly avenues in the ranks of the untrained rebels and soon the proposed attack became a horrible shambles. Two days later the duke was captured near Ringwood and taken before his uncle, King James I, where he grovelled at the royal feet and even offered to become a Roman Catholic in return for a pardon. The king, having rather enjoyed the spectacle, sent him to the Tower where he was beheaded on 15 July.

This was not enough for King James. He determined to make a terrible example of all those who had supported the duke in his attempt to usurp him. For his instrument of revenge he chose Judge Jeffreys, 1st Baron of Wem.

In Taunton Jeffreys conducted the Bloody Assize in the great hall of the castle, sentencing over 200 local men to the gallows and condemning others to slavery in the West Indies. The women who, such a short while ago, had danced gaily with Monmouth's lieutenants were whipped.

The music in the Fiddler's Room is thought to go back to the night when the duke's followers hailed him as their king, the tramp of feet being those of the soldiers who dragged the captive rebels to face the wrath of the Hanging Judge. Two visible ghosts also haunt Taunton Castle. One is a man dressed as a cavalier who, holding an antique pistol, appears on a certain landing. The other is a young woman dressed in the fashion popular at the time of the Monmouth Rebellion.

Visiting Information

Situated in St James Street, Taunton, Somerset. Open daily.

THIRLWALL CASTLE

The legend of Thirlwall owes as much to folklore as ghostlore but it is still a good Border story. The first record of the castle, built of stones plundered from Hadrian's Wall, goes back to 1369. Its picturesque ruins make a wonderful setting for its traditional guardian, a fabled black dwarf.

For several centuries the castle was the home of the 'Fierce Thirlwalls' and the legend was born when the crusading Baron John de Thirlwall returned triumphant from some distant war. He brought with him a baggage train of loot, the pride of which was a table cast of solid gold. Its guardian was a hideous dwarf whose ebony skin proclaimed that his origin was as exotic as that of the table.

The fame of the golden table of Thirlwall spread across the Border country. Raids were carried out by envious Border lords eager to seize the treasure for themselves. But it was the Scots who finally managed to enter the castle and slay its defenders.

When the victors battered down the heavy door of the chamber where the table was supposed to stand, they found that it and its

Thirlwall Castle.

guardian had vanished. For a moment the raiders stared about the empty room, cursing with chagrin.

Then one of the party rushed in with news that the last of Baron John's surviving retainers had glimpsed the dwarf just as the castle was captured. He was staggering to the castle well under the weight of the fabled table. Here he flung it down the shaft and then jumped after it.

The Scots raced to the well but when they arrived in the courtyard they found the paving stretched from wall to wall without a break. The genie of the table had magically sealed the well opening and – it would be nice to think – guards his table to this day in some subterranean cavern far below the castle's foundations.

Visiting Information

Situated a mile north of the village of Greenhead, Northumberland. Freely accessible.

TINTAGEL CASTLE

There is something about the legends of King Arthur and his knights that has rooted deep in the British imagination. Although there is debate as to whether Arthur ever existed, it is most likely that the real Arthur was a Celtic leader who rallied his people against the invading Saxons and who developed cavalry into such an effective weapon that the foundation was laid for the stories of the armoured Knights of the Round Table.

The story of the king as it is told today is based on Sir Thomas Malory's *Morte D'Arthur*, published by Caxton in 1485, which glorifies the brave virtues of Arthur and his Knights, and tells of their quest for the Holy Grail, the mystical chalice which once held the blood of Christ.

According to Malory, Arthur was the son of King Uther Pendragon and Igraine of Cornwall. Magic enters the story describing how Merlin magically transformed Uther into the likeness of Igraine's husband Gorlois, Duke of Cornwall, so he could spend a night with her while she was besieged at Tintagel Castle where their son was to spend part of his childhood.

The castle, which stands on a rocky headland on the Atlantic coast of Cornwall, was built in 1145 by Reginald, Earl of Cornwall and illegitimate son of Henry I. The fact that it was built in the twelfth century does not rule out possible Arthurian connections with the site as Celtic remains are there dating back to the fifth century.

The present ruins make an ideal setting for the Arthurian legend and were the inspiration of Tennyson. His *Idylls of the King* achieved such fame that it inspired a public subscription to maintain the ruins in 1852.

Over the centuries there was a belief that the spirit of King Arthur periodically returned to his birthplace but a more curious local tradition was that twice a year the whole castle disappears and briefly materialises in some strange fairy realm.

Visiting Information

Situated on a headland overlooking the sea, the castle ruins are close to the village of Tintagel, Cornwall. Open at weekends.

TIVERTON CASTLE

The tragic ghost of Tiverton Castle met her untimely end within a few hours of being married. The castle goes back to 1106 when it was raised by command of Henry I, and then enlarged two centuries later and there were modifications in the sixteenth century. Later it was bombarded into surrender during the Civil War by Sir Thomas Fairfax.

According to tradition the cause of the haunting goes back to a long ago wedding when the younger guests at the marriage feast decided it would be fun to play hide-and-seek in the castle. While music played and wine flowed the older guests looked on with amused tolerance as the players rushed about searching for places to hide themselves.

Tiverton Castle.

The bride joined in and came upon a long massive coffin-shaped chest with elaborate carvings. As it was empty she decided it would make an ideal hiding place. She climbed in, lay down and gently lowered the lid above her. When the bride heard the seeker at the door of the room, she allowed the lid to drop the final inch. Immediately a spring lock snapped into place and she could no longer hear the festive sounds of the party. She must have waited a few minutes before she tried to push up the lid only to find she was trapped.

When the game was over the guests went about the castle vainly calling her name. No one thought of opening the great old chest. It was locked so how could she have got inside.

What had begun as a game became a tragedy as no trace of the missing bride was found. The mystery was not solved until much later when the lid of the old chest was opened and her remains were seen in her fading wedding dress.

Visiting Information

Situated in Tiverton, Devon, close to the local church. Open from Easter to end of October.

TOWER OF LONDON

In 1196 'for moving the common people to seek liberty' William FitzAskert was imprisoned in the Tower of London before being 'by the heels drawn thence to the Elms in Smithfield and there hanged'. In 1747 Simon Fraser, Lord Lovat, became the last prisoner in the Tower to be beheaded for his part in the Jacobite Rebellion in 1745. During the 531 years between these dates the shadow of the Tower fell across the political life of England, a chilling reminder of the penalty of offending authority.

Members of the nobility as well as commoners have met their fate in this palace fortress and some of their ghosts have returned there. Among the spectres that over the years have been reported as returning to the Tower are Edward V and his brother, Lady Jane Grey, Lord Northumberland, Lady Salisbury – who tried to flee from the headsman – Sir Walter Raleigh, Guy Fawkes plus less recognisable apparitions. William the Conqueror entrusted Gundulf, Bishop of Rochester, to build the White Tower in 1078 because he deeply distrusted London's 'fierce populace'. Nineteen years later the rectangular keep of Caen stone, erected on the south-east corner of London's Roman Wall, was finished and at various times was used as a palace, a fortress and a prison.

In 1234 Henry III built the great hall and the Wakefield Tower and to improve the overall appearance had the castle white-washed, thus giving it the name of the White Tower.

Near the site of the causeway across the moat, by which the Tower is still entered, a menagerie was once situated in the Lion Tower from which has lingered the ghost of a bear.

One midnight in January 1816 a sentry on guard outside the Jewel House saw a figure like a great bear appear at the door of the regalia room. Instinctively he raised his musket and lunged at the animal. The weapon passed through the animal and the point of the bayonet was embedded in the door behind it. The apparition advanced menacingly on the soldier who collapsed in a faint.

Edmund Swifte, Keeper of the Crown Jewels, wrote: 'I saw him once again on the following day, but changed beyond recognition. In another day or two the brave and steady soldier, who would have led a forlorn hope with unshaken nerves, died at the presence

The Tower of London.

of a shadow.' Swifte also experienced a mysterious paranormal phenomenon which was described in *Notes and Queries* for 1860.

> I was at supper with my wife in the Jewel House which is said to have been the doleful prison of Anne Boleyn. I had offered a glass of wine to my wife when she exclaimed 'Good God! What is that?' I looked up and saw a cylindrical figure like a glass tube about the thickness of my arm, hovering between the table and the ceiling. Its contents appeared to be a dense fluid, white and pale azure.

According to Swifte this lasted two minutes before pausing over his wife's right shoulder whereupon she shrieked, 'Oh Christ! It has seized me!'

The strange object then disappeared as mysteriously as it had come and Swifte declared, 'Even now while writing, I feel the fresh horror of that moment.'

The phantoms of Edward V and his younger brother Richard – the Princes in the Tower – have been glimpsed at various times over the last five centuries in the Bloody Tower where tradition tells that their uncle Richard III was responsible for what Sir Thomas More described as 'the dolorous end of these babes'.

Unfortunately these two pale spectres have not given a clue to one of the great mysteries in English history – what was their real fate.

The only evidence against Richard III for their murder was given verbally by Henry Tudor, nearly two decades after he had usurped Richard's throne.

On 19 May 1536, Queen Anne Boleyn was led out to Tower Green for her execution after being found guilty of committing adultery with her own brother and casting spells on Henry VIII.

After calmly ascending the scaffold, she made a brief speech in which she accused no one of her death and while she did not acknowledge the crimes of which she had been charged, expressed submission to the law. Her head was then struck from her body by an executioner brought from Calais as decapitation by the sword was a French custom not practised in England until then.

The day after the execution King Henry married Jane Seymour. Anne's body was interred in the Tower's chapel of St Peter ad Vincula (St Peter in Chains) and it is here that her spectre has appeared. The chapel was used as a burial place for the more important prisoners executed in the Tower. Queen Victoria took an interest in it and had the floor taken up so that the human remains there could be identified and given proper burial. Over 200 bodies were found but only a few could be named.

One night an officer making a tour of inspection saw a light showing through the chapel's clear windows. He questioned the

The Tower of London.

sentry about the cause of this and the soldier told him he did not know but he had noticed it before.

The officer was so intrigued that, being unable to enter the locked church, he propped a ladder against the wall, climbed up and looked in through a window. He saw a number of people in old-fashioned costumes walking in a mournful procession down the aisle. At their head walked a woman who resembled paintings of Anne Boleyn that the officer had previously seen. The phantom promenade continued up and down for several minutes, then the figures vanished and darkness returned to the church.

Anne Boleyn is also reported to haunt Tower Green, where she was one of seven prisoners who were given the privilege of being executed there instead of providing a spectacle for the London mob at Tower Hill. Sometimes she is seen walking towards the White Tower and at other times only footsteps are heard.

The validity of this can be gauged by an incident which occurred one night in 1864. A soldier was found lying unconscious by his sentry box. To be asleep or drunk on guard duty is obviously one of the most heinous military offences, and the man was brought before a court martial.

He told the tribunal that when he saw a white figure approaching out of the darkness he shouted a challenge. As the figure still advanced, he raised his rifle and then saw that the form before him was a headless woman. Two other witnesses gave evidence supporting the soldier's statement with the result he was acquitted.

Visiting Information

The nearest underground station is Tower Hill, about a three-minute walk to the castle entrance. By rail it is a twenty-minute walk from London Bridge station, and by river access from the Tower Pier. Open daily.

TRIERMAIN CASTLE

All that remains of Triermain Castle – also known as Gilsland Castle – is a ruined tower standing on a grass-covered mound in a field close to Hadrian's Wall in Cumbria, yet its pathetic ghost is famous among Border legends.

The first Norman fortress to be built in the district, it was originally surrounded by a moat and comprised four towers enclosing a courtyard. Built with stone from a nearby quarry which had first been worked by Roman engineers, it was originally owned by the de Vaux family. In 1340 Edward III granted a licence for the castle walls to be crenellated. Such royal permission was required for the fortifying of a building in order that only those approved by the king could maintain a stronghold.

During the savage politics of Elizabethan times, Triermain's lord was attained and lost his estate and castle. A contemporary document stated, 'Tradermayne was sometimes a fair castle, a house of great strength and of good receipt; and was a very convenient place, both for annoying of the enemie and defending the country thereabouts; but now the said castle is utterly decayed.'

So it remained until interest was rekindled through Sir Walter Scott's poem *Bridal of Triermain*. The poet, who was inspired by Border legends, wrote:

> Where is the maiden of mortal strain,
> That may match the Baron of Triermain?
> She must be lovely and constant and kind,
> Holy and pure and humble of mind …

The poem tells how Sir Roland de Vaux, Lord of Triermain, found his ideal in the person of Gyneth who he rescued from Merlin's enchantment. The tomb of the real Sir Roland is to be seen in the nearby Lanercost Priory.

Apart from the *Bridal*, Trierman has another claim to legendary fame. It is the home of a sad spectre well known as the Gilsland Boy who haunts the castle's surroundings. A small invisible and icy hand seizing yours is the way he usually manifests himself. When his shade has been actually seen it has been described as a frightened-looking

Triermain Castle.

child with chattering teeth who stretches out his hands as though imploring food. Legend tells that the boy was the victim of a wicked uncle who saw him as the only obstacle to inheriting the castle after he was orphaned. One freezing day in the depth of winter the uncle took the unhappy heir out on to snow-covered Thirlwall Common where he deliberately lost him. The terror of the abandoned child in the swirling snowflakes is disturbing to imagine. It was several days before his frozen body was found where he had vainly tried to shelter by a rock.

According to local legend he appeared whenever a descendant of his uncle was about to be taken ill. If the illness was to prove fatal the ghostly boy would lay his ice-cold hand on the affected part and whisper, 'Cauld, cauld, aye, cauld. An' ye'll be cauld for evermair.'

Visiting Information

The ruined tower of the castle stands 3 miles to the west of Gilsland, Cumbria. On farmland but the tower can be seen from the road.

WARKWORTH CASTLE

The doomed hero of Warkworth Castle on the River Coquet was Sir Bertram of Bothal who owed fealty to Lord Percy of Alnwick, known in history as Hotspur.

Before leading an attack on his long-standing enemy Earl Douglas, Hotspur held a banquet at Alnwick Castle. To it was invited the Lord of Widdrington and his beautiful daughter Isabel who looked with a fond eye on handsome young Bertram.

During the festivities a minstrel sang of bold knights and chivalrous deeds, and Isabel, responding to his Arthurian epics, later sent her maid to Bertram carrying a helmet with a golden crest. The message was implicit. When he had won the right to wear the helmet through deeds of valour, such as the minstrel described, she would be his.

Soon Bertram had the opportunity to prove himself. Hotspur's force crossed the river and clashed with Douglas' Scots warriors. His head full of Isabel and the gold-crested helmet, Bertram plunged into the thick of the battle and was badly wounded. When the mauled raiders withdrew, Bertram was taken to Warkworth Castle to recover from his wounds. Here he impatiently waited the arrival of Isabel. Her father, having seen the battle, had promised to describe the young knight's gallantry to Isabel and allow her to travel to Warkworth to nurse him.

After several days passed and there was no sign of the ministering angel, Bertram left his sickbed and journeyed with his brother to find out what had become of Lady Isabel. They reached her father's tower at dusk. An old woman, once the nurse of Isabel, appeared and explained that six days ago her mistress had set out for Warkworth. Fearing that Isabel might have come to harm on the way, Bertram disguised himself as a minstrel and rode north in search of her. His brother set off in a different direction.

After several days the despondent young man was resting beneath a hawthorn tree when a friar came by and was struck by the melancholy expression on Bertram's face.

According to an old ballad he said:

> All minstrels yet that e'er I saw
> Are full of game and glee,

Warkworth Castle. (stock.xchng)

> But thou art sad and woebegone,
> I marvel whence it be.

Sir Bertram explained his quest, hoping that the wandering monk might have news of his lost Isabel. The holy man replied:

> Beyond yon hills so steep and high,
> Down in a lonely glen,
> There stands a castle fair and strong
> Far from the abode of men.

He added that when he had been passing this castle he had heard the voice of a maiden lamenting from a turret window.

Bertram hurried to the castle and kept watch on it from a nearby cave. After nightfall a moonbeam illuminated the turret the friar had described and he saw the face of Isabel at an embrasure. He spent the next day in his cave trying to think of a way to rescue her.

On the third night weariness overtook him and he slept until dawn. When he opened his eyes he saw Isabel leaving the castle by means of a rope ladder. Holding it steady by the castle wall was a young man in the costume of a Scot. Aghast that Isabel could play him false with this youth, Bertram followed the couple until they were out of sight of the castle. Then, drawing his sword which he had secreted under his minstrel's cloak, he rushed at the Scot with the words 'Yield that lady or die.'

The young man drew his claymore and the clash of steel was accompanied by Isabel's anguished cries. A moment later the Scot was on the ground and as the knight prepared to give him the *coup de grace* the girl threw herself over his prostrate body.

'Stay, 'tis thy brother,' she cried.

Her words came too late. The sweep of the blade could not be halted and it ran into her breast. Although she was dying, she managed to whisper to Bertram how his brother, disguised as a Scot, had found her in the clutches of a reiver and had arranged her escape.

Soon afterwards a band of men from the castle found the stunned figure of the English knight standing dumbly by the bodies of his sweetheart and his brother.

They seized Bertram and held him until Hotspur ransomed him from his captors and sent him to Warkworth to get over the tragedy. But the grieving knight never did. He gave his gold-crested helmet and his possessions to benefit the poor, then quit Warkworth for a spot on the banks of the nearby Coquet.

Here in the cliff above the river he hewed out a hermit's cell and a little chapel where he could meditate and pray for the souls of those he had killed. Over the arch of the chapel he carved the words: 'My tears have been my meat and drink day and night.'

Sir Bertram, now known as the Hermit of Warkworth, spent his life there and on occasions after his death his sorrowing shade has been seen standing by the Coquet close to the remains of his chapel.

Visiting Information

Situated 7½ miles south of Alnwick, Northumberland. Check website for up-to-date information.

WARWICK CASTLE

The original fortification was built on the present site of Warwick Castle before the Norman Conquest by Ethelfleda, the daughter of King Alfred. The present castle goes back to the fourteenth century. For a long period it was owned by the Earls of Warwick who were very active politically often to their downfall. For example, one of the earls was Richard Neville, known in history as 'the King Maker'. He was killed at the Battle of Barnet in 1471 and Warwick Castle went to George, Duke of Clarence, who had married Neville's daughter Isabel. He was found guilty of treason seven years later and was said to have been drowned in a butt of malmsey wine.

However, the castle ghost was not in the king-maker class; he was an Elizabethan poet. Fulke Greville, 1st Baron Brooke, was an Elizabethan poet who wrote over a hundred sonnets as well as a couple of plays. He also served as a Privy Councillor. James I conferred the castle upon him and he restored it at great expense to 'the most princely seat within the midland parts of the realm' which is still a good description of Warwick.

In 1628, while in London, Sir Fulke was stabbed by a hitherto trusted servant named Ralph Heywood. He committed suicide afterwards but Sir Fulke lingered a month before death overtook him. Then his restless spirit returned to his castle which he had lovingly renewed. There the haunted room was Sir Fulke's study where he continued to make his eerie presence felt.

Another supernatural story concerning Warwick Castle appeared in Volume 14 of the regular publication *Notes and Queries* in 1918:

An ancient dame had the privilege of selling spare milk at the castle. She so cheated her customers that the earl hearing of it cancelled the privilege. She then bewitched the castle, usually in the form of a black dog. The chaplain and the vicars of St Mary's and St Nicholas brought the evil one to rest by reading passages of scripture, and eventually followed the witch in the form of a dog to the height of Caesar's Tower from which she or it sprang into the stream to a chamber prepared under the milldam. Her statue was placed above the tower battlements until blown down some years back.

Warwick Castle. (stock.xchng)

Visiting Information

Situated in Warwick, Warwickshire. Open daily.

WINDSOR CASTLE

Windsor Castle is the world's most famous castle. Before the Norman Conquest Edward the Confessor's Saxon palace was close to the present site. After 1066 William the Conqueror used it and then decided to build a Norman castle nearby and in 1086 it was entered in the Domesday Book. In the following centuries it has served as a royal residence and still does. With such an historical background, it is not surprising that the castle is reputed to be haunted by four royal ghosts.

Taking them in chronological order, they are Henry VIII, Queen Elizabeth I, Charles I and George III.

The invisible spirit of Henry VIII manifests itself aurally with the sound of weary footsteps as the king, who grew gross and dropsical towards the end of his life, drags himself painfully along a corridor. A sound of wheezing breath accompanies his painful struggle he suffered due to his ulcerated leg.

Probably the best known account of a Windsor haunting goes back to a day in February 1897. Then an officer in the Grenadier Guards named Carr Glynn was reading in one of the rooms of the Queen's Library when he saw a lady dressed in black walk out of an inner room and cross the chamber. He heard the sound of her shoes on the polished wood floor and he could have almost touched her as she walked past him and disappeared into a corner.

At first Lieutenant Glynn thought she must have gone through a doorway into another room. A moment later, one of the castle servants emerged from it and the lieutenant questioned him as to the identity of the dark lady. The man replied emphatically that no one had entered the room he had just left. Greatly mystified, the lieutenant then went into the room into which the lady had disappeared. It was empty and there was no exit by which she could have left.

The attendant then told him hesitantly that he must have glimpsed the ghost of Queen Elizabeth. She had been seen before, walking across the library in exactly the same way as the Guards officer described.

Standing in the castle's grounds is the Canon's House which has been revisited by the spectre of Charles I. Although a number of the historical ghosts who met their fate through the headsman's axe are

Windsor Castle.

said to appear in their decapitated state, the phantom of the tragic king is complete, the face being remarkably like the melancholy features depicted in his famous portraits.

The reign of George III was marred by his bouts of so-called insanity. Modern medical research suggests these bouts were not due to insanity but that he suffered from a rare disease known as porphyria, a blood disorder, which attacks the brain and nervous system and only came to be understood in the middle of the twentieth century

Despite the king's odd behaviour at times his malady did nothing to diminish the affection that so many of his subjects felt for him. They nicknamed him 'Farmer George' because of his interest in horticultural matters. His popularity can be gauged by the universal thanksgiving – and the monuments – which celebrated his returns to normal behaviour. But in the last decade of his life from 1810, when the Prince of Wales was appointed regent, the king was in a state of permanent mental derangement. He passed the lonely hours in a room in the castle playing on his harp. Now his shade returns to the apartment in which he was restrained.

Apart from royal ghosts, the most illustrious spirit to have manifested itself in Windsor Castle is that of Sir George Villiers, the father of the ambitious Duke of Buckingham. The duke was 'Steenie', the pampered favourite of James I, who became one of the most influential men in the kingdom. After the king died Buckingham retained his position of power through his friendship with the late king's son Charles I. As he continued to hold the same power over Charles as he had with his father, he became one of the most hated men in England.

Edward Hyde, 1st Earl of Clarendon, wrote in his *History of the Rebellion in England*, published in 1707, that Buckingham was so unpopular that predictions of his death became current. No doubt these were merely forms of wishful thinking, but Clarendon wrote, 'Among the rest there was one which was upon a better foundation of credit than usually such stories are founded upon. In February 1628 an officer at Windsor Castle woke one night to see a man of very venerable aspect who, fixing his eyes upon him, asked if he knew him.'

The startled officer's midnight visitor resembled the late Sir George Villiers. The ghost replied that he was right and he wanted him to go to the Duke of Buckingham and warn him that 'if he did not somewhat to ingratiate himself to the people, or at least abate the extreme malice they had against him, he would suffer to live but a short time.' Then the phantom faded away and the officer, thinking he had been the victim of a nightmare, drifted back to sleep.

The next night the ghost reappeared, and again asked the officer to go to his son with the message. Still the officer ignored the request, believing in the reassurance of the morning light that he was the subject of a recurring dream.

On the third night Sir George manifested yet again with the same request. The officer, now accustomed to these night visitations, answered that it would be difficult to get the duke to take notice of such a wild tale, whereupon the ghost confided in him 'two or three particulars' which he said he must not mention to anybody but the duke. Impressed at last that he had seen a real spectre, the officer rode to London and was admitted into Buckingham's household where he was conducted to the duke by Sir Ralph Freeman.

Afterwards the officer told Sir Ralph that when he spoke of 'those particulars which were to gain him credit', Buckingham went white and swore that the information had been known only to him. Having listened to the warning the duke went to his mother's house where they spent three hours talking excitedly. Clarendon wrote that when Buckingham left his mother 'his countenance appeared full of trouble'.

On 23 August of that year the duke was assassinated at Portsmouth by a discontented subaltern named John Felton who became a popular hero overnight. Clarendon concluded:

Whatever there was of all this it is a notorious truth that when the news of the Duke's murder was made known to his mother, she seemed not in the least surprised, but received it as if she had forseen it, nor did afterwards express a degree of sorrow as was expected from such a mother for the loss of such a son.

Another ghostly appearance is that of William of Wykeham, later the Bishop of Winchester, who designed the Round Tower which was added to the castle in 1348. At night his phantom has been seen looking up at his work with obvious satisfaction.

The long walk in the castle's Great Park was haunted by a less illustrious ghost. While on sentry duty there he committed suicide. A few weeks later a soldier saw the shadowy form of the young man in the moonlight.

The Great Park was also the scene of one of Britain's oldest and most spectacular hauntings. The vengeful ghost was Herne the Hunter who was immortalised in Harrison Ainsworth's book *Windsor Castle*. The legend dates back to the reign of Richard II when Herne was the King's Keeper of the royal forest.

One day the king was hunting when a wounded stag turned upon him and he would have suffered great injury had not Herne leapt upon the stag and dispatched it with his knife. In doing this he was badly gored and when his body was pulled away from the dead animal was clear he was desperately wounded.

At that moment a hermit with a reputation of wizardry appeared and told the king that if he agreed to his form of magical treatment he could save Herne's life. King Richard gave his assent and the stranger removed the stag's antlers and bandaged them to Herne's head. He then asked that Herne be carried on a litter to his hut in the forest where he would nurse him until he recovered.

As Herne was about to be carried away the king promised him that when he was well again he would be appointed the chief of the royal huntsmen. This created resentment among the rest of the hunters. They set off to the hermit's hut jealous and determined that the order of promotion should not be upset by Herne's appointment. They made it clear to the wizard that if he wanted to stay alive he must make sure that Herne did not recover. The wizard replied that Herne was under his guardianship and he could not harm him, but if the huntsmen dared to suffer Herne's curse he would see to it that Herne did not remain hunt leader for long.

The men laughed off the idea of a curse and were delighted to see that when Herne returned to the castle he seemed to suffer from amnesia as far as the Great Park was concerned. It was as though he had forgotten the woodland tracks along which the deer ran. Each hunt he led was doomed to failure. After several disappointing days of sport, the king lost his temper and dismissed Herne. That night, heartbroken by the disgrace, Herne hanged himself from the branch of a huge oak tree which, until 1863 when it was blown down during a gale, was known as Herne's Oak.

One of the hunters who had threatened the wizard to bring about Herne's downfall was walking near the oak when he saw Herne's body swinging in the wind. He rushed to tell the other hunters but when they reached the spot the body had vanished. From then on the misfortune that had befallen Herne befell them. Each hunt was a failure and the king was so furious at their unexpected ineptitude that they feared dismissal. They went to the hermit in the forest and he declared that until atonement was made to Herne's earth-bound spirit they would have no luck. Following his instruction they congregated round the oak at midnight whereupon the phantom of Herne, with antlers growing from his head, appeared. He commanded the terrified huntsmen to follow him.

Through the night the wild hunt, led by the horned ghost, combed the forest to drive away the deer with the result that when the king went hunting there were no animals left for his sport.

Realising there was something uncanny about the disappearance of game, he forced the story from the hunters. That night he went to the oak where Herne's ghost duly materialised and promised that if the huntsmen who had betrayed him were punished he would cease to haunt the wood as long as the king was to reign.

King Richard agreed and had the conspirators hanged, after which there was no difficulty in finding game. But following the king's murder in 1400 the ghost of Herne the Hunter returned to the Great Park.

Visiting Information

The castle dominates the town of Windsor, Berkshire. Open daily. As it is a working palace visiting arrangements may change at short notice and it is advisable to check the website before a visit.

INDEX